You _____ are about to create the life
you can't wait to live, and that will make you Better Than Good!

Better Than Good

Better Than Good

Zig Ziglar

THOMAS NELSON
Since 1798

NASHVILLE DALLAS MEXICO CITY RIO DE JANEIRO BEIJING

Library of Congress Cataloging-in-Publication Data

Ziglar, Zig.
    Better than good : creating a life you can't wait to live / Zig Ziglar.
        p. cm.
    Summary: "Better Than Good offers practical and spiritual vision for what life can be when
we allow the power of purpose and passion to permeate our soul"–Provided by publisher.
    ISBN-13: 9-781-59145-400-7
    ISBN-10: 1-59145-400-X (hardcover)
    1. Christian life. 2. Conduct of life. 3. Success–Religious aspects–Christianity. I. Title.
    BV4501.3.Z54 2006
    248.4—dc22
                            2005030299

I dedicate this book to my beloved son,
John Thomas Ziglar,
the president and CEO of Ziglar Training Systems.
Of him I am immensely proud.

Contents

Introduction

Not being one to shy away from introductions, let me tell you who I am and what you're going to discover in *Better Than Good.*

My parents named me Hilary Hinton Ziglar back in 1926 when I was born in Alabama, but ever since grade school my friends—and I hope that includes you—have called me Zig. For decades I've been traveling around the world speaking to audiences about getting the best out of life by putting your best into life. Whether in business, personal, family, or community settings, I've told millions of people that they can have everything in life they want if they will just help enough other people get what they want.

After seventy-nine years of living, twenty-plus books on motivational subjects, and countless speeches and seminars on living the abundant and fruitful life, I have more than ever to say. I feel like I'm just getting started! And that's why I've written *Better Than Good*—I've got some things to share with you that I believe will motivate you the same way they have motivated me. I've connected some dots between subjects I've addressed over the years that are creating new levels of motivation for me. And I want you to connect those same dots in your life.

I can't remember exactly when I said, "Better'n good!" the first time, but it was a long time ago. Being raised in the south and then living in Texas, I've participated in exchanges like this thousands of times:

"Hey, Zig! How ya doing?"

"Good, good. How 'bout you?"

Recognize those words? Nothing wrong with them, of course. They're just the colloquial way friends greet each other everywhere.

But at some point it dawned on me that "good" was not an apt description of how I was doing—or how any of us ought to be doing. If we're going to live life to the fullest, we ought to be doing "better than good." So that's why when people say to me, "Hey, Zig! How ya doing?" I respond: "I'm doing better'n good!"

The response has been amazing. People literally stop in their tracks to remark on my greeting. Some thank me for giving them a needed lift; others make my greeting their own. The power of words should never be underestimated. When you say, "I'm doing 'better than good'," that's a first person, present tense, positive affirmation of who you are and where you are. Just saying you are doing "better than good" won't make it so. But when you understand what it takes to live the "better than good" life and apply yourself, your life will truly be better than good.

There are three pillars to the "better than good" life: passion, peak performance, and purpose. I don't think anyone can stay motivated for very long in life without understanding all three of these concepts. And I don't think anyone will live a "better than good" life if he or she is not motivated to do so.

In essence, that brings me to the thesis of this book: the "better than good" life is experienced by living with genuine passion, striving for peak performance, and fulfilling one's God-given purpose. And I don't mind telling you up front: my goal is to motivate you to want to live that kind of life!

Here's how we're going to connect the dots between passion, peak performance, and purpose. I don't care what the field of endeavor is—sports, business, science, medicine, education, ministry, public service—I don't believe anyone will perform at his or her peak without passion. Life's too tough to get to the top without passion. You're going to fail, be taken advantage of, be disappointed by people you trust, disappoint yourself, run out of resources—almost every day you're going to encounter a good, solid, logical reason why you ought to give up. And without passion, you just might. That's why passion is the prerequisite for peak performance.

Peak performance is dependent on passion, grit, determination, and a willingness to do something poorly until you can do it well. True peak performance is influenced by the condition of your physical, spiritual, business, and family life. I address each of these areas in depth.

The third part of the equation—purpose—is something I have come to believe is a key to the whole dynamic of motivation and the "better than good" life. For years I've recognized that it's hard for a lot of people to be passionate about what they're doing because they don't like what they're doing! And it's hard to argue with that reality. There are lots of people who would rather be doing something different with their lives. When asked this question, "If obstacles were not an issue, what would you like to be doing with your life?" many people (most people?) don't say, "I'm doing what I know I was put on this earth to do. I wouldn't want to do anything else."

I admit that's a problem not easily solved. Because of family and financial obligations, it can be difficult to change course and start doing what you would rather do. Difficult . . . but not impossible. I believe if you truly have a passion for something—and if you believe it's your God-given purpose in life—you can do it.

And that's where we get to the discussion of purpose—what it is, how we find it, and the difference knowing one's purpose can make.

So when you arrive at Part III of this book—The purpose of the "Better Than Good" Life—we're going to talk about something that not a lot of motivational speakers talk about. And I include myself in that list—for the early part of my career, but no longer. I know what affirming my own purpose in life has done for me in recent years. It's why I said earlier that I feel like I'm just getting started! There are large parts of my life's purpose yet to be achieved. As a result, I've never been more motivated! And I want you to be motivated as well—to live with passion and achieve true peak performance in that which you are convinced is your purpose in life.

I've met people all through my life who had passion of a sort. But because their passion wasn't fueled by purpose, it would come and go in bits and pieces. They were trying to generate their passion out of their own energy day after day, something that's ultimately unsustainable. Scientists have yet to invent the world's first perpetual-motion machine—everything runs down or runs out of gas eventually, including human beings trying to maximize their peak performance day after day.

If you had asked me in 1971 what my purpose was in life, I would probably have tried to say something impressive. But you couldn't have looked at my life and seen a lot of purpose—or at least not the kind of purpose I talk about in this book. Truth be told, my career was going nowhere; my finances were a mess (translation: I was broke!).

But all that changed beginning in 1972. That's when I discovered what it means to grasp true passion in life—passion that fuels peak performance and leads to purpose for a lifetime.

What happened? Simply, yet profoundly, this: I had an experience that ignited passion in me and convinced me I was uniquely created for a special purpose. (If we were talking together personally, you'd probably say at this point, "Tell me what happened, Zig!" You can read more about my experience in the epilogue to this book.) Suffice it to say that *Better Than Good* is my best effort at bringing together who I am and what I've learned over the last thirty-plus years about living a life that is "better than good."

I've made this book as practical as I can. I'm going to give you ideas along the way that have worked for me (and for thousands of other people) through the years. Things like this: use an electronic notepad or buy yourself a pack of 3 x 5 cards and keep them handy while you're reading this book. When you read something that speaks to you—an idea, a thought, a plan, a value, a reason, a correction—jot it down. Then carry those cards with you wherever you go. When you have the opportunity—stuck in traffic, on hold on the phone, waiting in a doctor's office, before going to sleep at night—review your notes. Try this for the next thirty days. Change takes time and constant repetition. Feeding your mind new ideas for at least a month is like practicing scales on the piano—you're teaching your mind and body how to do things they've never done before. In time, you'll do them naturally. But until then, stay motivated with your 3 x 5 cards or electronic notepad.

I'm convinced that *Better Than Good* can help motivate you to connect the dots in life, little by little. The end result will be a picture of beauty, purpose, and fulfillment.

My prayer is that you will discover God's true purpose for your life—a purpose that ignites passion and peak performance. Whether you discover that purpose for the first time through this book, or have that sense of purpose renewed, I believe this book will help you create a life you can't wait to live—a life that is "better than good!"

PART I:
THE PASSION OF THE "BETTER THAN GOOD" LIFE

1 | A Passionate Journey

Experience shows that success is due less to ability than to zeal. The winner is he who gives himself to his work body and soul.
CHARLES BUXTON

Blind zeal is soon put to a shameful retreat, while holy resolution, built on fast principles, lifts up its head like a rock in the midst of the waves.
WILLIAM GURNALL

The core problem is not that we are too passionate about bad things, but that we are not passionate enough about good things.
LARRY CRABB

Passion, for all its dangers, needs uncaging if we are to move towards completeness as human beings.
PHILIP SHELDRAKE

Men spend their lives in the service of their passions instead of employing their passions in the service of their life.
SIR RICHARD STEELE

P assion is underrated and underrewarded. When a student with an average IQ performs magnificent feats in the academic world, give passion the credit. When you see an athlete with only average ability accomplish herculean tasks, give passion the credit. When you see a parent provide for his or her children despite physical or educational handicaps and roadblocks—obstacles that would stop an ordinary person in his or her tracks—give passion the credit.

American independence was won because of the passion of our founding fathers. Every religious revival has had passion as its source. The American civil rights movement was fueled by the passion of Martin Luther King Jr. and other civil rights leaders. Passion deserves far more credit than the records of history provide.

I believe passion plays a significant part in all great accomplishments. Who—and Whose—you are will determine whether your passion is noble and generous or selfish and self-serving. Finding and developing passion is a journey, not an event. There is a process you must follow; some find it early, while some discover it much later. A noble passion, when found and developed, produces great joy and personal rewards and offers huge benefits to society as well.

I am going to tell you the stories of two passionate people who came from very limiting backgrounds—people whom, had you and I looked at their circumstances, we might have passed over as incapable of peak performance and success. But we would have been wrong. The passion they developed in their particular fields of expertise illustrates the point that passion is cultivated and developed over time for most people. Reading their stories will encourage you to believe that passion is lurking in you just waiting to be released and give you examples of how to set it free.

A Dream That Wouldn't Die

Different things motivate different people, but inspiration is critical if we are going to discover what we are passionate about. Author Debbie Macomber's inspiration came from an unusual source: the death of a much-loved cousin who succumbed to leukemia. They had been especially close for many years, and David's death had a profound impact on Debbie. After the funeral she said, "It seemed as if God was saying to me that I could no longer push my dreams into the future, which I had done for years with a long list of excuses and justifications. I was one of those people who was going to do it when . . ." David's death showed her that later doesn't always come, that today is the time to pursue one's dreams.

Though she didn't realize it at the time, a defining moment had occurred before David's death when she went to see him at the cancer center where he was receiving treatment. As a dyslexic, she had difficulty reading the directional signs and finding her way into the hospital. After wandering around in frustration for a while, she stopped a doctor and asked him for directions. His answer changed her life. He said, "Go all the way down this corridor and take the first right. Then walk through the doors marked 'Absolutely No Admittance.'"

Debbie says now that she has spent the rest of her life walking through closed doors—because she discovered that day that she could.

High school had not been easy for Debbie and she was unable to secure a scholarship for college. So she did what many young women did in the 1960s—she married and had four children in the next five years. As a stay-at-home mom she dreamed of one day writing books but never thought it would be possible. Today she is convinced she would have continued to do nothing more than dream had it not been for the death of her cousin. She talked it over with her husband and he agreed she should give writing a shot. So she rented a typewriter and put it on the kitchen table, moving it at mealtimes.

In telling her story today, Debbie emphasizes the fact that she has no background that qualifies her as a writer. Her parents were children of immigrants; her father never finished high school and was a POW during World War II. To this day she identifies herself as a "creative speller" and affirms she has no credentials as a writer other than the dream she believes God planted in her heart. She believes dreams come from Him and that the only way we have a prayer of them ever being fulfilled is if we turn to Him in faith and belief.

While the kids were off at school during the day, Supermom turned into a struggling young writer. "Rejections came so fast," she said, "I [felt] that sometimes they'd hit me in the back of the head on the way back from mailing off another proposal at the post office." Her list of rejections was impressive, but after five long years she finally got her first book published.

Debbie heard me speak at the Tacoma Dome in 1990. She said my talk blew her away and had a significant impact on her. She realized she had only reached the tip of the iceberg when it came to becoming a successful author. At that time, her books were in the stores for a few short weeks after releasing, and she would joke that they had the shelf life of cottage cheese. Print runs were limited, and there was no possibility she would make any of the recognized best-seller lists.

Debbie Macomber refused to follow the popular trend of writing about immorality and sex in her novels, saying she didn't want her books to dishonor the standards of the Bible. "Each of my stories was what was characterized as a traditional or sweet romance," she said. "After hearing you, Zig, I realized that all things are possible. You made a believer out of me."

At that seminar Debbie bought nearly all of the books and

tapes I had for sale—about eight hundred dollars' worth. She and her husband listened to all the tapes and studied the books. She has told me that she thinks God guided her to the seminar that day to give her the inspiration and encouragement to believe she could pursue her passion of writing—and be successful.

Are you ready for this? Today Debbie has seventy million books in print worldwide and her royalties have risen many times over since she first started listening to those tapes. Her books have been on every major bestseller list, including the *New York Times* hardcover and mass-market paperback lists. "People often comment that they appreciate my clean style—they aren't afraid to pass my books along to their grandmother or their children," she says.

Debbie still listens to the tapes she bought in 1990, and when I'm in town she comes to hear me. Not long ago she took The Redhead (that's what I affectionately call my wife, Jean, when I'm talking about her—I call her Sugar Baby when I'm talking to her) and me to dinner. She says God has given her a means of imparting positive words and messages to her readers through the power of stories. I believe her assessment: "God has given" is the foundation of the passion for what she does. Once she took her eyes off making those all-important sales figures and focused on her message, the one she believed God gave her, she started achieving the success she had been seeking.

Debbie considers attending our Advanced Training Program to be the most important thing she did along her journey to success. She knew the course was demanding, fun, and thought provoking and offered twenty-four weeks of follow-up. However, as much as it appealed to her, her life was too busy. She fought the battle of balance as many people do, and trying to fit in one more thing seemed counterproductive. But she did it anyway and found a means for creating the balance that had eluded her.

Today she has precious grandchildren and structures her time to be with them. Her entire family traditionally spends the Fourth of July together. They've even taken an Alaskan cruise to celebrate the July holiday in honor of her deceased father who so loved America. She and her daughters hold a Gratitude Tea every year for the people who have blessed their lives as a way to thank them and let each one know how special they are.

When I think of Debbie Macomber, I think of a passage of Scripture that, rendered in the modern vernacular of *The Message* translation, describes Debbie to a T: "Live creatively, friends....Make a careful exploration of who you are and the work you have been given, and then sink yourself into that. Don't be impressed with yourself. Don't compare yourself with others" (Galatians 6:1, 4).

While she is one of the most passionate people I know, Debbie has not become "impressed with herself," which is what makes her passion so attractive and infectious. She is a down-to-earth mother (now grandmother) who had a dream and decided to go for it, struggling for years to create a niche for herself in the market, all the while balancing her passion for her dream with her commitment to her children and husband. She is living proof that dreams do come true when they are fueled by a passion that serves others and honors God.

Against All Odds

The passionate people who make the greatest contributions to society are not only highly motivated—they have proper motives. And, in the final analysis, proper motives always seek to accomplish goals that contribute to the common good . . . that serve others . . . that make the world a better place. The only way to move up from a place of mere survival to stability, and from stability to success, and from success to significance, is to engage in a God-inspired field of endeavor that will enable you to bring significant benefits to others. George Washington Carver did just that— and he did it against great odds.

If George Washington Carver had done nothing more than survive his own childhood, he would have qualified for honorable mention on the list of the world's great achievers. He was born in January in the early 1860s on a farm near Diamond Grove, Missouri. The Carvers (from whom George derived his surname) were German immigrants who had come to America and settled in Missouri. They were not fond of slavery, but it seemed the best way to secure help and companionship for Susan Carver, who was unable to have children.

The Carvers had a slave named Mary who gave birth to two sons, the second of whom was named George Washington. (The father was a slave from a neighboring farm.) While just a baby, he and his mother were kidnapped and taken to Arkansas by bushwhackers, who often stole and resold livestock and slaves from the isolated farms of the Ozarks. Mr. Carver pursued the thieves with no success, but upon his return offered a big reward for the mother and her child. Within days the exhausted and weakened baby George was returned for the reward, but his mother, Mary, was never heard of again. The boy's father was permitted regular visits but tragically died in a farm accident a few years later.

Without the loving care of Susan Carver it is believed that baby George would have died when he developed a severe cough and was barely able to breathe. Although he survived, his health was never strong, and the residual scars of his early illness gave his voice an awkward quality that many found difficult to understand.

Here was a youngster who had all the odds stacked against him: born into slavery, orphaned, suffering from ill health and childhood difficulties. But he was undaunted by obstacles.

Carver's natural, God-given fascination with the whys and wherefores of life started him on a lifelong quest for knowledge. At age ten he left the security of the Carver farm to attend a Negro school in a nearby community. Not knowing where he would stay or how he would live, he just knew he had to go, and so he did.

This started the passionate journey that would take him from town to town and state to state, until he was able to study and teach at the highest levels.

To his great credit, George Washington Carver never lost his innate fascination with the mysteries of life. With a humble faith, early in his career he asked God to reveal to him the secrets of the universe. In his own humorous way, he noted that God told him the secrets of the universe would be beyond his range of expertise. However, God said, He would reveal to the young scientist the secrets of the peanut. That sense of humor carried Carver through many years of painstaking research into the lowly tuber.

Carver made his way to the Tuskegee Institute in Alabama, founded in 1881 by Booker T. Washington. Carver was hired to head up the department of agriculture, his responsibilities being to teach, lead, and inspire the students and the departmental faculty. But his love of research—his passion for investigating the secrets of the universe—kept him in the lab instead of the classroom. Washington finally gave in to Carver's passion for exploration and created a department of agricultural research over which Carver would have complete control.

Though he no longer had primary teaching responsibilities, the students at the Institute would not be denied his influence. They begged to have classes with him, so contagious had his passion become. One summer, while he served on the staff of a youth conference, a large group of boys would get up before five in the morning every day to accompany him on his early morning walks. Like a benevolent Pied Piper, Carver led them on walks that revealed to them the beauties and intricacies of nature. Every created thing was a source of wonder to him. Things the average person would walk by or step on or over, Carver would pick up and explain in fascinating detail. One young member of that conference recalled Carver stopping and picking up a common weed, explaining how its antiseptic juice could be used to seal up wounds incurred while shaving.

The inspiration he provided awakened a thirst in his students for even greater knowledge—the mark of a true leader. Many applied to study under him. If they were white students, it was impossible, since Alabama law made it illegal for whites and Negroes to study together. But they could write to him—and they did. And he answered, busy though he was. After one youth conference, seven boys wrote him 904 letters.

Of course, it was not just curiosity that attracted people to Carver. His discoveries of nature's mysteries also proved useful. He taught southern farmers, black and white alike, to rotate their crops instead of planting only cotton year after year. When his advice made peanuts so plentiful that the bottom fell out of the market, he went to work to discover new uses for this otherwise novelty plant. He developed more than three hundred synthetic products from peanuts, including milk, butter, cheese, coffee, flour, breakfast food, ink, dye, soap, wood stains, and insulating board.

To demonstrate the peanut's versatility, he had his class serve Dr. Washington and other staff members a five-course meal made entirely of peanuts. The menu was soup, mock chicken, peanuts creamed as a vegetable, bread, ice cream, cookies, coffee, and candy. The only item that did not contain peanuts was a salad of peppergrass, sheep sorrel, and chicory.

His research led to so many discoveries that entire industries were changed forever. Consequently, he was offered thousands of dollars for his discoveries, but refused to profit financially from his laboratory work. He turned down Henry Ford's offer of a six-figure salary, as well as the offer of a $175,000 salary from another company.

As a result of all his accomplishments, Dr. George Washington Carver was arguably the greatest scientist of the nineteenth century. His strong faith in God was his guiding light throughout all of his full life. His passion to discover everything he could about everything God had made, including the peanut, made his life a nonstop source of excitement not only to himself but to countless others. George Washington Carver never grew bored with life, because he saw it as an infinite object of investigation and an endless source of discovery. He was the kind of person for whom passion was a given and service was a constant. He lived to make the lives of others better.

A Passion to Make a Difference

I close by pointing out that there is passion and then there is passion. Some people have passion that rarely is exercised beyond the bounds of their own experience. They get great satisfaction and enjoyment from that which is their pursuit. But it remains a self-indulgent passion, if you will.

There are others whose passion is to change the world with that which they dream about. Debbie Macomber didn't just want to write. She wanted to write stories that were wholesome and edifying; stories parents could give their children to read and feel good about; stories that would remind older readers of the classic fiction of past generations. In other words, she wanted to use her passion to write to make a contribution to families just like her own. So that's what she did. She wrote and wrote, mailed off proposal after proposal, weathered rejection after rejection . . . until finally she got published. And tens of millions of books later, she's still at it—fulfilling her passion by making other people's lives more fulfilling at the same time.

George Washington Carver did the same. He believed that since God created the world on purpose, there was no part of His creation that was without a reason for its existence. He believed everything in nature had a benefit, and it was his passion to discover as many of those infinite benefits as one lifetime would allow. He saw his passion and abilities as gifts from God, not for sale to the highest corporate bidder. He saw himself as a steward—a manager of the abilities he had received from on high. It was his responsibility to use those abilities—to exercise his passion for research into nature—to benefit the widest audience possible. And that's what he did, humbly and joyfully, his whole life.

That's why I say there is passion and then there is passion. I believe the highest form of passion is that which sees the greater good as its object. The "better than good" life is lived by those who have passion for changing the world they live in. It might be just their own family, their neighborhood, their church, their company, their community, or their nation they touch. But ultimately, to impact just one person with our passion is to change the world. To encourage, inspire, and motivate one person with our passion is to move beyond ourselves and take others with us. That is the essence of the "better than good" life.

If you have a passion (there is no one who doesn't, even if they haven't yet discovered it), don't give up on it. Find a way—ask God to show you the way—to turn your dreams into reality. When you do, you'll be living the "better than good" life.

2 | Inspiration: The Fuel of Passion

As I grow older, part of my emotional survival plan must be to actively seek inspiration instead of passively waiting for it to find me.
BEBE MOORE CAMPBELL

Listen to the voices.
WILLIAM FAULKNER

Ninety percent of inspiration is perspiration.
PROVERB

You can't wait for inspiration. You have to go after it with a club.
JACK LONDON

Do not quench your inspiration and your imagination; do not become the slave of your model.
VINCENT VAN GOGH

It usually happens that the more faithfully a person follows the inspirations he receives, the more does he experience new inspirations which ask increasingly more of him.
JOSEPH DE GUIBERT

A nyone who ventures into the wilds of Alaska or fishes in the salmon-rich rivers of British Columbia or goes hiking in the pristine wilderness of the great American West—that person is told one thing by guides, park rangers, and experienced outdoorsmen: whatever you do, don't put yourself between a mother bear and her cubs. There is a man in Dallas, Texas, who probably wishes he had heeded that advice before tangling with a mother who surprised him with her passion for protecting her children. The July 15, 2005, issue of the *Dallas Morning News* told the dramatic story.

Antelma Arroyo, with her three young children in the car, had stopped at a gas station in Oak Cliff, a suburb of Dallas. As she was standing outside the car pumping gas, a man approached her and demanded her purse. When she refused, the man jumped into her car with the intent to steal it. This protective and passionate mother flew into action. She screamed at her children to get out of the car. Javier Frias, the six-year-old, made it out while Mrs. Arroyo pulled four-year-old Adriana Frias out. But eighteen-month-old Alondra Frias was still strapped in the car when the man began pulling away.

So the purse snatcher-turned-carjacker gunned the engine and peeled out of the gas station with Mrs. Arroyo running alongside fighting for control of the steering wheel. He hit the street and picked up speed, but Mrs. Arroyo wouldn't let go of the steering wheel. She was being dragged along the street on the outside of the car with the carjacker punching her in the face trying to make her let go of the steering wheel. Somehow she was able to pull herself in through the driver's window of the car, still fighting with the man who was trying to drive off with her eighteen-month-old. In the confusion, the guy stalled the car, decided he'd had enough of this mother, and fled the scene.

Man, I wanted to shout, "You go, mama!" I'm betting that guy will think twice before putting himself between a mother and her baby again. He had no idea of the passion that seemingly mild-mannered mom was prepared to unleash on him. Think about it—she didn't prepare for that event, she had no warning, she hadn't practiced it and would never have predicted that's how she would respond.

But that's the true nature of passion! It's continually simmering beneath the surface, waiting for the right stimulus to cause it to boil over into world-changing action.

Physics and Passion

I believe inspiration is the fuel of passion. If you think of passion as the flame that burns white hot in the heart of every person, inspiration is the fuel that keeps that flame alive.

Often I meet people in whom the fire of passion seems to have gone out. You can see it in their eyes—there's no spark or life! It's like someone came along and flipped off the passion switch while they weren't looking. The big mistake is thinking that regaining passion is a passive event—something we just have to wait for until we're moved once more to become passionate about life. Not so! Passion is a flame that has to be fed in order to keep it burning bright. And inspiration is the fuel that keeps the fire alive.

Who is responsible for feeding inspiration to the flame of passion? You are! And if you don't, trust me—passion will, over time, become a distant and only occasional visitor to the house of your heart.

Give me this one short paragraph to be scientific. As I understand it, physicists use a law—the Second Law of Thermodynamics —to describe a fully documented bit of reality about our world. Here's the law: in a closed system, entropy (disorder) increases. That means that the amount of thermal energy available to do work decreases. Energy decreases, disorder increases. Now, in Texas terminology we'd say it this way: stuff wears out, breaks, and runs down unless you constantly do something to keep it in working order. Without injecting new energy into the situation, things naturally go from a state of repair to a state of disrepair. (Leave a car in an open field and come back and check on it in ten years. It doesn't get better; it gets worse.)

Now, that law applies not only to "stuff" but human beings. The ultimate expression of that law is that, regardless of how many vitamins and nutrients we pump into ourselves in old age, we die physically. But we also die spiritually and emotionally if we don't constantly inject and invest new energy into our spiritual life. *Passion will die without constant injections of new inspiration.* And you and I are responsible for inspiring ourselves; we are responsible for keeping the flames of passion burning strong.

There's a verse in the Bible that speaks directly to this issue. The apostle Paul had a young pastor-protégé named Timothy, to whom he wrote a couple of letters of advice and instruction. Timothy may have had a passive kind of temperament as a young man based on these two verses Paul wrote to him: "And for this reason I remind you to kindle afresh the gift of God which is in you through the laying on of my hands. For God has not given us a spirit of timidity, but of power and love and discipline" (2 Timothy 1:6–7).

I have been taught by those who know the original Greek language of the New Testament that the word *kindle* is in the present tense—meaning "keep on kindling." It's not a once-in-a-lifetime event. Rather, it's a lifelong responsibility for us to stir up and rekindle the gifts God has given us. We're not to be timid about it either. We're to be proactive about the passions, the dreams, the desires we believe God has put in our heart. For Timothy, it was being a pastor. For me, it's being a public speaker. And for you, it's . . . (you fill in the blank).

The question is, what are you doing to continually rekindle the passion of your life? What kind of inspiration are you providing for yourself that will keep you pursuing your dream? And if that passion dies, who's to blame?

If you take one thing from this chapter, let it be the application of the Second Law of Thermodynamics to your spiritual and emotional life: passion will die without constant inspiration.

In the rest of this chapter, I want to give you four practical ways to inspire yourself—to feed the fires of passion burning within.

1. INVEST IN INSPIRATION

When people consider where to give some of their income for charitable or nonprofit purposes, they often think this way: "Gee, I don't feel very passionate about any of those causes, and I want to really feel strongly about what they're doing if I'm going to give my money to them." Have you ever heard that? Have you ever said that yourself?

We think, "Where my heart is, there will my money be also." But Jesus said, "For where your treasure is, there your heart will be also" (Matthew 6:21). If you treasure your money, you probably won't be giving much of it away. But if your heart gets involved as a result of coming to know the people you've been asked to help, you're much more likely to support them financially as well as physically and emotionally.

Do you see the difference? One view says, "When my heart kicks into gear (i.e., when I feel passionate), I'll invest my resources." But the correct view is, "I'm going to get involved because familiarity will increase my awareness, and once relationships are established I'll want to invest more than just my time and energy." The fastest way I know to build and develop your passion in a given area of life is to invest your time, talent, and treasure in it.

Take Antelma Arroyo, the mother in Dallas I told you about. Now don't misunderstand what I'm saying here about the reasons she fought to defend and protect her children, and especially her baby still strapped in the car seat, from the carjacker. But those children were her most valuable earthly possession. She had invested years of blood, sweat, and tears in the raising of her precious brood. She, like any mother would, displayed a passion for protecting her children that was completely commensurate with what she had invested in them.

I'm not placing a monetary value on a mother's love—saying she fought for her children because of what she had invested in them in a monetary sense. How can one put a price tag on a mother's love—the agony of labor and delivery, the sleepless nights of nursing a sick child, the sacrificing of her own wants in order to provide for her children's needs? Her investment in her children was incalculable, and as a result so was her passion to rescue them from harm.

You and I have three kinds of resources given to us by God that we can invest in whatever we choose: time, talent, and treasure. God doesn't come down and dictate to us every morning how we are to use our time, apply our talents and abilities, and spend our money. From our human point of view, He leaves those choices to us. But I can tell you this: the more of your time, talent, and treasure you invest in your passion, the more you will fight for it, defend it, and protect it from everyone and everything that would attempt to steal it from you.

Let's say your passion is to own your own flower shop someday. Right now, you're not involved with flowers except as a hobby and impressing your neighbors with your gorgeous gardens every spring. But the children have left the nest and you know the time is right to make this move—to give wings to your passion. If I were to come to your house and spend an hour talking with you about your passion, I'd be looking for signs that you're investing your time, talent, and treasure. I'd be looking for bookshelves full of books on flowers and running a small business, magazine subscriptions on the same subjects, your class schedule for the course on entrepreneurship and small-business management that you're taking at the local community college, check stubs from your payment of dues to the appropriate floral associations, your applications to several local flower shops where you plan to work as an apprentice for the next year or so in order to get experience, the syllabus from a success and motivation seminar you recently attended . . . and on and on.

It's pretty easy to tell when someone is, and isn't, investing in inspiration. I've never met anyone yet who was living his or her passion—I mean "pedal to the metal"—who was not a heavy investor in inspiration.

2. INQUIRE FOR INSPIRATION

Many people today don't realize this, but there was a time when lawyers, doctors, and other professionals (not to mention trades-people) learned their skills by studying with a mentor. Lawyers, for example, "read law" with a practicing attorney until they knew enough about the law in their community or state to become qualified to practice. The loss of education by apprenticeship is one of the sad results of our modern, classroom-based educational systems.

Do you want to keep your passion alive? Find a mentor—someone who has the same passion—and make some kind of arrangement to meet with that person on a regular basis for inspiration. There is nothing more inspiring to me than meeting with someone who is already successful at what I have a passion to do. Inspiration is caught better than it is taught.

Let's go back to Mrs. Arroyo again. The Latin cultures are famous for something I wish Americans were still famous for—their sense of extended family. And I have no doubt Mrs. Arroyo was part of an intergenerational chain of instruction where the passion for little *niños* and *niñas* was passed from grandmothers to mothers to daughters to granddaughters *ad infinitum*. Those of you who have had the privilege of experiencing the benefits of an extended family environment know what I mean. Under normal circumstances there are no classes given on parenting—it's a hands-on, on-the-job training environment. The passion for family and children is caught, not taught. Learning is by example, not by explanation.

When that kidnapper-carjacker tried to make off with her baby, the passion inspired by Mrs. Arroyo's extended-family cultural values kicked into high gear immediately. She wasn't just fighting for her baby; she was fighting for the value placed on babies by all the mentors she had likely been exposed to in her culture—grandmothers, aunts, her own mother, cousins.

There is no better way to stay inspired than by spending time in the presence of inspirational people. There is a healthy sort of peer pressure that keeps pushing us forward, a symbiotic effect that causes us to become more in the group (even a group of two— you and your mentor) than we could ever become by ourselves.

One of my favorite Bible verses about the dynamic of healthy church life says, "Let us consider how to stimulate one another to love and good deeds . . . encouraging one another . . . " (Hebrews 10:24–25). There is no substitute for the "one another" environments in life. King Solomon said that just as "iron sharpens iron, so one man sharpens another" (Proverbs 27:17).

How do you find a mentor—someone to inspire you and help keep your passion aflame? In short, you ask. Obviously, you have to first find someone who is doing what you want to do, and preferably someone who does it well, shares your values, and has plenty of experience. Then, you ask. There are other resources available on mentoring relationships that you can read. But it boils down to your courteously inquiring as to whether this person would agree to spend a set amount of time with you on a regular basis to impart what he or she has learned about "the business"— whatever it is you have a passion to pursue. You'll be surprised how many people—especially retirees—would love nothing better than to have an outlet for imparting the passion they've been pursuing for decades.

Find someone inspiring and attach yourself to them, but only if you follow Zig's Golden Rule of Apprentice-Mentor Relationships: don't become an apprentice unless you're willing one day to be a mentor yourself. That's what happens naturally in extended families. Apprentices grow up to become mentors—and it's the way passions stay alive for generations.

3. GET INVOLVED TO FIND INSPIRATION

To use an obvious example, what could have been more inspiring (and fearful!) to the English Separatists who left England in the early 1600s than the idea of moving to a sparsely populated continent to begin a new life? What could have been more inspiring to America's founding fathers than beginning a new country? What could have been more inspiring to millions of European immigrants sailing into New York's harbor than to see the Statue of Liberty welcoming them to their new home? And what could have inspired an entire nation of Americans—men, women, and children—to live sacrificially for the decade surrounding World War II more than the call to save their beloved homeland and Western civilization at large from a Nazi madman who threatened to take over the world?

Sometimes we have to get up and get involved in order to find inspiration and keep passion alive. And the bigger the movement is in which we choose to get involved, the more inspired we are. Which inspires you more—being the only person sitting in a football stadium or being one of seventy thousand screaming fans who are just as excited as you are about the home team?

I speak to crowds of tens of thousands of people at a time. And I can tell you from my own experience, I am always more inspired after I speak than I am before. The bigger the crowd, the more inspired I am. Why? Because I feed off the energy of the twenty thousand people who are looking for the same things in life I'm looking for: success, inspiration, encouragement, and motivation.

When people spend their money to come hear me speak, I know they're serious. And when thousands of them do it, it makes me grateful and excited to give it everything I've got.

If your passion is golf, invest some of your time and treasure being part of the gallery at a major tournament. Mix with the crowd, *ooooh* and *ahhhhh* over the good and bad shots, and watch the pros' every technique. You'll be more fired up about your golf game after identifying with the thousands of other people in your area who are also passionate about golf.

If you're passionate about writing, attend writers' conferences and the large trade meetings where new books are displayed annually. Join a local writers' group (or start one), attend book signings and readings, and volunteer to serve at a literary festival or at your public library.

Whatever your passion, get involved in it at a level that is bigger than you are—like Antelma Arroyo did. She became part of something that was bigger than she was when she became a mother. There were three little ones that day who looked to her, depended on her, and expected things of her—and it was up to her not to let them down. When you become part of something bigger than you are, you become accountable. You become inspired to do your best. You become motivated to not let others down. And that fuels your passion in ways that can't be described—it can only be experienced.

4. IMAGINE FOR INSPIRATION

I can well imagine that Antelma Arroyo, like every mother, spent untold hours daydreaming about what she wanted for her children: education, health, good jobs, loving spouses, and plenty of grand-babies for her to spoil one day. The power of the imagination is one of the greatest untapped resources in the human tool kit. It's amazing that mental images have such power—but they do.

One of the things that spurred me on as a rookie speaker was my imagination. I pictured myself speaking before crowds of thousands of people, knocking them dead with my humor and wisdom and humbly receiving their standing ovations. That didn't happen overnight, but I never allowed that picture to be erased from my mind. And eventually, everything I had imagined, and then some, became reality.

Bruce Barton made an interesting observation: "I do not like the phrase 'Never cross a bridge until you come to it.' It is used by too many men as a cloak for mental laziness. The world is owned by men who cross bridges on their imaginations miles and miles in advance of the procession. Some men are born with more of an imagination than others, but it can, by hard work, be cultivated—not by mere daydreaming, not by lazy wondering, but by hard study and earnest thought."

To this very day I still imagine exactly where I will put the emphasis on a word, how long I'll pause between this statement and that, if I'll raise or lower my voice, and if I'll raise my arms or get down on one knee to make a point while I'm speaking.

As I arrange my notes, I'm deciding at what point in my presentation I'll walk from one side of the stage to the other, how fast I'll do it, and how long I'll stay there. My imagination helps me work through what I want to be the best speech I've ever given. It is as Bruce Barton says, hard study and earnest thought, but the results are well worth the effort.

Please understand I speak of the imagination only in the way I believe God intended it to be used: as a source of inspiration and motivation. I am not into New Age beliefs that suggest we can create reality just by thinking hard enough about it. I believe God created reality and how I respond to Him determines my condition in life. But I believe the pictures we paint for ourselves of the kinds of things we'd like to achieve can be powerful stimulants.

One thing that motivates me tremendously about spending my eternity in heaven is how I imagine it will be. God allowed the apostle John to have a glimpse of heaven that he transcribed in his book of Revelation. I can read portions of John's descriptions—which I believe to be true—and get an idea of what to expect. I'm sure I've imagined some things incorrectly, and that's fine. But I know I have imagined the grandeur, glory, and gladness of heaven correctly, which is one reason I'm so passionate about my faith.

God's Word gives me many details about the life of Jesus Christ, but few details about His physical appearance, and I imagine what He might look like when I encounter Him in person. I can't wait to meet Moses, Noah, Matthew, Paul, and other heroes of the faith about whom I have created mental images based on the facts I've read. It's the hope of heaven that the Word of God has promised, and what I imagine based on those promises that makes me long to go there.

Whatever your passion is, turn your imagination loose and let it inspire you to keep working to make your dreams become reality. Remember: it's your job to fuel your passion, and inspiration is the fuel you need.

I've given you four ways to keep the flow of inspiration strong in your life—and I imagine you've thought of others as you've read. When you inspire yourself to keep your passion alive, you'll be like the proverbial mama bear and her cubs: nothing in this world will be able to separate you from the object of your passion. The result? Peaks of performance you've never reached before.

3 | Stress: The Enemy of Passion

He has honor if he holds himself to an ideal of conduct though it is inconvenient, unprofitable, or dangerous to do so.
WALTER LIPPMANN

Blessed is the man who is too busy to worry in the daytime and too sleepy at night.
EARL RINEY

All worry is atheism, because it is a want of trust in God.
FULTON SHEEN

The only thing we have to fear—is fear itself.
FRANKLIN DELANO ROOSEVELT

There is no such thing as a minor lapse of integrity.
TOM PETERS

With the fearful strain that is on me day and night, if I did not laugh, I should die.
ABRAHAM LINCOLN

The enemies of passion will steal every good thing you possess if given the opportunity. Your money, your reputation, your integrity, and your family are all at risk. Not only can they steal your passion, they are also capable of stealing your joy, your dreams, and your purpose for living.

The thief I see robbing more people of their passion than anything else is stress—stress in all its forms. That happened to a man who ended up in Houston, Texas, after bailing out of his life for seven years due to stress.

Ed Greer had a white-collar job with the Hughes Aircraft company in El Segundo, California, in the early 1980s. But he was miserable. He hated his work and was under various kinds of pressure from his wife and father about issues in his life. One of his coworkers reported that Ed told him one day, "Never become too good at something you hate. They'll make you do it the rest of your life." (How's that for evidence that something had stolen Ed's passion?)

Ed wasn't willing to put up with the stress of a job he hated and relationships that were wearing him out. So, on September 10, 1981, he simply disappeared without telling anyone. He flew to Ft. Lauderdale, Florida, where he lived on the beach and supported himself by fixing boat engines. In time, he assumed another person's identity and moved to Houston where he got a job with a small oil exploration firm.

After several years his wife divorced him *in absentia* and he became somewhat of a legendary hero to multitudes of yuppies who felt trapped in corporate America but didn't know what to do about it (more cases of stolen passion). His former coworkers at Hughes Aircraft even began holding annual celebrations in his memory, somehow thinking there was something noble about a guy who threw in the towel in the game of life.

Finally, seven years after he disappeared, the FBI caught up with him. The then forty-year-old dropout explained to the media, "I felt trapped. I didn't like my life."

Life 101

Stories like Ed Greer's make me think of the uninspiring message I used to see on bumper stickers a few years back: "Life is hard. Then you die." It's true—life is full of stress. It takes someone deluded or in denial to believe that it's not. Therefore, the question is not "How do we avoid stress-producing situations?" but "How do we learn to live without succumbing to stress?" And more specifically, in terms of the message of this book, "How do we keep stress from stealing our passion?"

People who are living the "better than good" life are people committed to maintaining passion for living. To maintain our passion we have to be realistic about the enemies of passion— those experiences, forces, and people who are looking for opportunities to steal our "better than good" life.

Let's be honest—life is hard. And I sympathize with Ed Greer and anyone like him who finds himself in a job he hates and in relationships that are unfulfilling. But he did the wrong thing. Bailing out is not the answer. I dare say that living with the guilt of what he had done, both morally and legally, created stress equal to what he had experienced before.

I read a lengthy article in *Reader's Digest* once that documented that 90 percent of all doctor's visits can be attributed, directly or indirectly, to stress. Stress suppresses the body's immune system, interrupts your sleep, and makes you vulnerable to all manner of illnesses. You get sick and experience a whole host of other problems related to missing work and the inability to fulfill other responsibilities—and that just leads to more stress. It's a downward cycle that rarely has a happy ending.

To be fair, let's say the actual number was only 50 percent instead of 90 percent of illness related to stress. Can you imagine the impact on this nation if half of all doctor's visits were cancelled as a result of people learning to eliminate stress from their lives?

Productivity would skyrocket, money would be saved, people would be happier—the impact would reverberate throughout society like ripples on the surface of a pond.

I'm not suggesting that all stress is bad. Stress in the form of adrenaline can cause us to flee burning buildings and jump out of the way of oncoming traffic. It can also cause us to work hard to complete a project before a looming deadline. Some stress can be good. But when it is too frequent and meets with no resistance from us, it can destroy us by stealing our passion.

The message of Life 101 is that life is stressful, but stress can be managed so it doesn't rob us of our passion. I'm going to give you six ways to defend yourself against the attacks of stress.

1. Wait to Worry

At the risk of sounding simplistic, this is something many people overlook. It's been my experience that most people are so used to living with stress they don't even know it—they're unaware of the specific things causing their stress. Like Ed Greer, they think a job you hate and unpleasant relationships are just part of life.

Take worry for instance. Most people spend so much time worrying that it never dawns on them that their worry could be producing stress and stealing their passion. They think worry is as normal as breathing—something you do if you're alive.

I've heard my friend and mentor Fred Smith talk about worry many times. Here is a summary of what he says about identifying the source of worry in our lives:

In 1942 I was a professional worrier. I mean, not an amateur. An amateur will take his worries and go to bed. But if you go to bed with your worries you run the risk of going to sleep. And when you wake up you've lost your self-respect. I mean, you just know you've lost your standing as a genuine worrier when you find out you've been asleep. Nobody who sleeps can qualify as a genuine worrier. No, if I got in bed and discovered that I had something to worry about I'd get up and sit in a rocking chair. I'd make myself a cup of coffee and sit there and rock. Eventually I'd go back to bed, but I wouldn't go there to sleep; I'd go there to perk. And I'd just lie in bed and perk.

In 1944 I conquered worry. I spent two years of intense work on the problem of worry. I figured out what I was afraid of: I had a better job than I really deserved. I was not qualified for the job I had. And I started worrying about losing it. Then I said to myself, "Well, wait a minute. When do you do your best work? When you're not worried." Well, if you can't hold your job when you're not worrying, how in the world can you hold it when you are worrying?"

I ended up writing three little words on the inside of my skull. If you ever perform a craniotomy on me, you'll find them right there: WAIT TO WORRY. I found out I was doing my worrying before I had all the facts; I was free to wait to worry. As soon as I had the facts I had all the information I needed to work out a plan. When you have a plan, you don't have anything to worry about, so I'd stop worrying. I learned to wait to worry.

My wife, Mary Alice, would be at the kitchen sink and she'd hear a yell in the front yard. She'd go to the front door to see what happened to the poor yard guy, and by the time she got there he had picked himself up and was already back to work. She'd go limping back to the kitchen sink and I'd say, "Honey, you've done enough worrying between that kitchen sink and the front door to fill the Empire State Building! Why don't you wait to worry?"

When our children were teenagers and weren't home

by the time of their curfew, Mary Alice would be convinced there'd been a car crash and that we'd soon be getting a call from the hospital. Then the kids would come in a few minutes late and I'd remind her, "Let's wait to worry."

Fred is right—waiting is a lot less stressful than worrying. The next time you are attacked by stress, identify the source. Many times you will discover you are worrying about something that doesn't need to be worried about at all. Once you get all the facts, you may be glad you waited.

2. Stay in the Game

Bonnie St. John Deane was a participant in the Paralympics. She was a one-legged skier who was competing against another one-legged skier. The other skier went first, and in the final run she fell. Bonnie confidently told her associates that she knew she was going to win because she wasn't going to fall. But she did fall and the other skier won. Bonnie's friends tried to console her by saying, "She was just a faster skier than you are." To this Bonnie adamantly responded, "No, she is not a faster skier. She just got up faster than I did."

I've never heard of anybody going all the way through life and not getting knocked down. Some people never get up and some get up so slowly it takes years and a lifetime of anger and bitterness before they recover. Bonnie St. John Deane assessed her circumstances correctly when she said, "People fall down. Winners get up. Gold medal winners get up fastest." Bonnie won the silver medal, was a Rhodes scholar, and became an award-winning IBM sales representative. She has been featured in *People* magazine, the *New York Times,* and *Ebony* magazine. With an attitude like hers, it's not surprising that she was once identified on *NBC Nightly News* as one of the five most inspiring women in America.

Getting up and getting back into the game removes the possibility of stress from long-term failure. Failure is not falling down—failure is not getting back up. Falling down is something that happened in the past. Regardless of what has happened in the past, if you are moving ahead confidently in the present, you have no cause to be stressed.

3. INSIST ON INTEGRITY

You can make a conscious decision in your life to do everything with integrity. When you do that, you inoculate yourself against any stress arising from guilt or shame. I've heard it said by many people that the great thing about telling the truth (living with integrity) is that you never have to remember what you said. If you're the kind of person who tells one person this and another person that, you're setting yourself up for big-time stress. You'll need to hire an assistant just to help you remember what stories you've told to whom. When you speak the truth, you speak and forget about it.

Removing relativity from your life is a great defense against stress. By that I mean some things in life are absolutely right and some things are absolutely wrong. There is black and white in life, and as soon as you agree with that you can relieve yourself of the stress that comes from trying to decide right and wrong every time a new situation arises. Our society today is buying into the idea that there are no universal truths—that what is right for me may not be right for you. That may be true when it comes to picking out the color shirt we're going to wear or car we're going to buy, but it's not true when it comes to honesty and integrity.

To point out the fallacy of relativism and its disastrous results, in public seminars I always ask this question: "How many of you would hire an accountant or a treasurer who admitted that he or she was just relatively honest?" Thus far I've never seen a business owner hold up his or her hand and admit, "Yeah, I'd be happy to hire a relatively honest accountant or treasurer."

We've been through a scandalous period in our country where many corporate leaders and accountants were found to be playing fast and loose with accepted principles of accounting. Trusting investors and employees lost millions of dollars when these accounting scandals were brought to light. Thousands of people lost their jobs and their retirement portfolios as well.

I've been happily married to The Redhead for fifty-nine years. We've celebrated fifty-nine honeymoons and are having more fun today than ever. In all the years I've been traveling and speaking, I've been away from home many nights. Not once when I've returned home has The Redhead asked me if I have been relatively faithful to her while I was gone. Nor do I ever expect her to. There are some things—like faithfulness—that are black-and-white issues.

In addition to integrity and relativity, when you grasp what Ralph Waldo Emerson said many years ago, that "ability without honor has no value," it gives you reason to pause and think. Not only that, he said, "If you would lift me up you must be on higher ground." This implies that if you are going to be in a position to help others get what they want in life you must have honor and integrity in your life. He capped it off by saying, "What lies behind you and what lies before you are tiny matters compared to what lies within you."

It's amazing how much stress you avoid when you play it straight. Do things with integrity, know what is wrong, practice what is right, and make your decisions accordingly. Your conscience will remain crystal clear, you'll live without regrets, and, as a result, your passion will remain alive and well.

4. STAY OUT OF DEBT

I'm going to borrow a verse from the Bible for this next point. In Revelation 3:17, Jesus issued the following evaluation of a particular church: "Because you say, 'I am rich, and have become wealthy, and have need of nothing,' [but] you do not know that you are wretched and miserable and poor and blind and naked."

This verse is a great illustration of how materialism can blind us to reality. We think we can become independent of God by virtue of our material wealth when in fact we are bankrupt to our true condition. In our race to keep up with the Joneses, we forget God and put ourselves under mountains of stress. We go into debt in order to keep up appearances and then worry because we can't pay what we owe.

People today say they can't afford to stay out of debt, as if it's a disease that has crept into their life without their permission. Fred Smith has reminded me that 85 percent of the conflicts in marriages today are caused by disagreements over finances. When he and his wife married, they were like most couples—they disagreed over finances! But they put a system in place that kept them out of financial trouble for more than six decades—and they started when Fred was making $208 a month. The first 10 percent of his gross pay went to God's work, and the second 10 percent went into savings. And they lived off of what was left.

"I must have it now!" is the battle cry of those who refuse to delay self-gratification. Oswald Chambers says that is the essential definition of lust—the belief that it is my right to have what I want when I want it. Couple the inability to delay gratification with the availability of everything we want or need, and match that with the painless purchasing plan of credit cards, and it is no wonder that the average American family now carries more than $9,000 in credit card debt.

Larry Burkett, the brilliant financial counselor, used to offer a three-part plan for staying out of credit card debt. I believe it still bears repeating and using:

1. Never charge anything on a credit card that you don't have money to pay for. In other words, use it as a charge

card, not a credit card. Following this rule will allow you
to . . .

2. Pay off your credit card debt every month.

3. The first time you fail to pay off your credit card at the
   end of the month, put your credit cards on a cookie
   sheet, heat the oven to 350 degrees, and put the cards
   in for thirty minutes or until they are nice and runny.

Anyone who follows that plan will never have to deal with the
stress of credit card debt again.

When I look at the financial burdens American families put
themselves under—thousands of dollars each year for activities
for their children, dues at clubs, huge car payments, living in
gated communities—I'm shocked. But I'm not surprised, then,
when I hear about the stress the same families are living with. The
never-ending quest to look good and feel good creates stress that
completely negates the attempt to create the perfect lifestyle. We
become hypocrites, trying to look good on the outside while dying
on the inside.

And who ultimately gets shortchanged in the deal? We do!
Because ultimately, Sunday morning becomes the time we devote
to ourselves to try to relieve some of our stress. "It's okay to skip
church. God wouldn't want us to be so uptight," we reason. So we
hit the golf course or the lake (spending yet more money we don't
have) in order to unwind. And we return home more wound up
than ever when we think of how we're going to pay for that brief
excursion into "relaxation."

No one can live a passionate life when he is worried about bill
collectors and bankruptcy. If you want to stay free of stress, stay
out of debt. It may take you months, even years, to get there. But
the freedom of being debt free will allow you to unleash your
passion in a way you'd forgotten could exist. And you'll discover
what the "better than good" life is.

5. FEAR NOT

I don't think most people are in touch with what they truly fear. I don't mean the fear of tornadoes or black cats or roller coasters. I mean the fears that lurk inside each of us that keep us from launching ourselves into the great adventure called life! We fear failure, of course—perhaps most of all. But we also fear losing the security of our own inhibitions. We fear losing control, and we fear the future. We fear living with the tension that exists between what we know and what we don't know—the security of the present versus the insecurity of the future. Some people just can't handle the unknown, so they remain bottled up, confined to the reality of the past instead of the potential of the future. Life is often like having one foot on the dock and the other foot on a boat that is leaving. We want to leave, but our desire for the safety of the homeland keeps us tentative and indecisive—and often lands us in the water!

Anything the Bible warns me about 365 times gets my full attention, and I've decided to take the words "fear not" seriously! Interestingly enough, fear and faith have something in common: each expects something to happen in the future. We just don't know what it is. What we do know is that what you expect is what is likely to happen. If fear is the dominant force in our life, we inadvertently—through unexplained actions and events—seem to attract disaster. On the other hand, if faith is the dominant force, it seems to bring about some good things because what we expect, we inadvertently work to achieve. The following story identifies the difference in the results of faith or fear put into practice.

You may remember the 2002 Winter Olympic Games when sixteen-year-old Sarah Hughes skated her way to a gold medal. She stepped on the ice not believing she had a chance of winning any medal, so she just decided to—as the kids say—"let it all hang out." She skated with reckless abandon, unconcerned about the live audience, the television audience, or for that matter, the judges.

She just gave it all she had. That sheer abandon she exhibited expressed the total joy she was feeling at the time and she turned in a spectacular performance, winning the gold.

You may also remember that Michelle Kwan skated after Sarah and was expected to win the gold. She was a true champion, beloved by skating fans the world over, and the recipient of many medals in her career. But after Sarah Hughes's flawless performance, Michelle went out determined not to make any mistakes. She fell, and she took the bronze. I've always felt that while Sarah was focused on what *to* do, Michelle was focused on what to *avoid* doing. And it made the difference. The fear of failing inhibits and restricts performance and can throw cold water all over human passion.

Did you know the opposite of faith is fear? When Jesus and His disciples were caught in a storm on the Sea of Galilee, the disciples were beside themselves with fear of drowning. Jesus asked them, "Why are you timid, you men of little faith?" (Matthew 8:26). We have two choices for facing the future: we can face it with faith or with fear. The future is all about the unknown, and we can let that empower us or enslave us.

The greatest fear of the future held by many is the fear of death. I remember immediately following the events of September 11, 2001, people asked me how my travel schedule would be affected. I said, "Not at all." I live my life looking through the windshield, not the rearview mirror. I believe the words of Psalm 139 that say the days of my life were ordained before I even existed (see verse 16). If that is true—and I believe it is—then no terrorist can touch me until God grants permission. Nor can any other harm befall me. And when it is my time to be promoted to heaven—regardless of how it happens—do you think I live in fear of that hour? Why, heaven is what I'm living for on earth! Until one has conquered the ultimate fear—the fear of death—no lesser fear is worth worrying about.

I encourage you not to be stressed about the future. We may

not know what the future holds, but we definitely know Who holds the future. Your faith in God will allow your passion to be boundless.

6. HAVE THE FIRST LAUGH

If all that talk about death in the last section stressed you out, then you definitely need what I'm about to say: passion is no laughing matter, but I've never met a truly passionate person who didn't love to laugh—out loud and with great gusto!

At my public seminars, I almost always conduct a little experiment on this subject. After speaking for a while on the subject of stress, I'll launch into a couple of lengthy stories that I don't have space to reproduce here. They have great punch lines and always draw gales of laughter from the audience. And then I ask the audience: "How many of you feel less stress now than when I started this talk?" One hundred percent of the time almost every hand in the audience goes up.

Why? Because laughter is a great stress reducer. If you have never read Norman Cousins's account of his experience of self-healing as described in *Anatomy of an Illness,* I encourage you to do so. When diagnosed with an incurable illness, he brought a movie projector into his hospital room and watched reel after reel of old classic comedy movies, laughing himself into hysterics. He found he could relieve his otherwise significant pain on a consistent basis through laughter. That practice, along with some other novel therapies, resulted in his healing. He left his prestigious journalistic career and taught on the faculty of a major medical school about the power of the mind and emotions in healing the body of disease.

Next to love, laughter has been described as the second most powerful emotion we can express. It has been said that laughter is like internal jogging—it stimulates the respiratory system, oxygenates the body, relaxes tense muscles, and releases pleasure-producing chemicals in the brain. You cannot laugh and be mad, laugh and be tense, laugh and be stressed. Laughter is low calorie, caffeine free, and has no salt, preservatives, or additives. It's 100 percent natural and one-size-fits-all.

Laughter is truly God's gift to humankind. You can get high on laughter but never overdose. Laughter is contagious—once it starts, little can be done to stop it. Laughter never felt bad, committed a crime, started a war, or broke up a relationship. Laughter is shared by the giver and the receiver. Laughter costs nothing, and it's nontaxable. Laughter is a trendsetter. If we can find ways to laugh first thing in the morning, it may in fact set the tone for the rest of the day.

Let me close by telling you the most important use of laughter I have ever discovered: the ability to laugh at ourselves. I stopped taking myself too seriously years ago, and it was the best decision I ever made. Don't get me wrong—I'm still serious about what I do. But not so serious that I can't be the first one to laugh when I mess up (which happens all too often—it's why I spend so much time laughing!). When you're the first person to laugh at yourself, you leave little room for others to laugh at you.

I don't know what your stress level is at this moment. It could be high—as I said at the beginning of this chapter, life offers up plenty of stress-inducing situations. And every one will attempt to rob you of a key ingredient in the "better than good" life: your passion. Don't let it happen. If you will wait to worry, get up when you fall, live with integrity, live debt free, face the future with faith instead of fear, and be the first to infect others with laughter— your life will be a Stress-Free Zone.

And when stress decreases, passion is free to increase. And your life is free to become "better than good."

4 | Watch What You Think

You are not what you think you are. What you think, you are.
UNKNOWN

For I say, through the grace given unto me, to every man that is among you, not to think of himself more highly than he ought to think; but to think soberly, according as God hath dealt to every man the measure of faith.
ROMANS 12:3 KJV

We can't choose our relatives, but we can choose our thoughts, which influence us much more.
UNKNOWN

The vague and tenuous hope that God is too kind to punish the ungodly has become a deadly opiate for the consciences of millions.
A. W. TOZER

Change your thoughts and you change your world.
NORMAN VINCENT PEALE

D r. Bruce Wilkinson, the well-known author of *The Prayer of Jabez* and other bestsellers, talks about motivating people to learn in his series for teachers, *The 7 Laws of the Learner*. He relates how a note scribbled on a paper he had written in graduate school com-pletely changed his perception of himself—and changed his future.

Bruce was in seminary where he took as many classes as he could from Dr. Howard Hendricks, the renowned professor of Christian education, public speaker, and leadership coach. A day came when Dr. Hendricks was to return to the class a paper they had written on some subject, and Bruce was anxious to see the grade his mentor had given him. When he received his folded paper, he slowly opened it just enough to see the grade: A+. He breathed a sigh of relief, then opened it the rest of the way and saw something that shocked him far more than his perfect grade. Scrawled with his traditional purple felt-tip pen was this note from the professor: "Bruce—I believe you have the potential to become one of this generation's greatest Bible teachers."

When Bruce tells this story in public, he has the audience laughing with him as he demonstrates how he walked home from class that day—holding the paper with Dr. Hendricks's note out in front of him in both hands, cradling it like it was the Holy Grail. He floated upstairs to his apartment to show his wife what Dr. Hendricks had written to him—and the rest is history. Bruce Wilkinson did go on to become one of America's greatest teachers and communicators not only of the Bible but on a host of other subjects as well. And he will tell you that a brief note from an esteemed professor was what put the thought in his mind that he might one day learn to communicate effectively. Given Bruce Wilkinson's prolific output and fruitful impact over the years, I would say Dr. Hendricks's note paid off in spades!

How Are You Doing?

Did you know that what you think powerfully impacts who you are? What you think about yourself, what you think about the world, what you think about others, what you think about your prospects in life—*everything* you think has an impact on the kind of person you will become.

For instance, conduct a little research of your own. For the next week, pay special attention to how people answer the question "How are you?" or "How ya doin'?" That question gets asked and answered millions of times each day—in fact, you probably answer it yourself more than once every day.

Listen to the answers people give to describe how they're doing:

"Not bad."

"So-so, I guess."

"Pretty good."

"Fantastic!"

"Terrible!"

"So far, so good."

"Not bad under the circumstances."

I'm going to guess that for every strong, positive, optimistic answer you hear from people you'll hear eight or ten that range from neutral to pessimistic. If people really are doing as poorly as I hear them say they're doing, I'm not sure why they get out of bed!

As I said earlier in this book, for longer than I can remember, I've been answering the "How are you?" question with something like, "Why, I'm doing better than good!" I answer that way because I truly expect things to be and become "better than good." I have learned through the years that, for reasons I can't scientifically or even theologically explain, how I expect things to be greatly influences how they become.

Our old friend Job, in the pages of the Old Testament, is a good example of this truth. After his family, property, and health had been destroyed through one disaster after another, Job confessed, "For what I fear comes upon me, and what I dread befalls me" (Job 3:25). Job lived in fear of God taking away everything he had—and it happened! It was all ultimately restored to him, but for a time Job's life was a self-fulfilling prophecy. Fear is an open invitation to trouble whereas faith invites success.

Is it wrong to say, "I'm doing better than good" all the time? Is that disingenuous? Absolutely not! Through the prophet Joel in the Old Testament, God called His people to prepare for battle, telling them, "Let the weak say, 'I am a mighty man'" (Joel 3:10). Is it wrong for one who is weak to say he is strong? Not if he has every expectation of becoming strong, which the people of God did when they had God on their side in battle. That's exactly how I look at life—that God is on my side when I live my life in a way that honors and pleases Him.

When Jesus said, "With God all things are possible" (Matthew 19:26), that means things are "better than good." When the apostle Paul says, "I can do all things through Him who strengthens me" (Philippians 4:13), that means things are "better than good." How could they not be when God is on our side?

Because "better than good" is such an optimistic approach to life, I guarantee that you will be remembered when you say that's how you're doing. And it will catch on! Nothing is as infectious as optimism and a positive outlook. For instance, I attend a church with twenty-five thousand members in Dallas where I teach a large Sunday school class. Because I've been replying, "I'm doing better than good" for so many years, many of the members of my class, as well as the church staff, have adopted it as their own reply to "How are you?" And I can see the twinkle in their eye when they say it, because I know they mean it.

I want to tell you about how the lives of some people changed when they began to change their mind and their outlook on life.

"Better Than Good" Business

Lisa Spicer moved from New Jersey to Frisco, Texas, near Dallas.

She was a single mother of three teenaged boys with no job and no health insurance. Things got worse when she slipped and broke her leg in two places—not a great beginning in what was to be a new start for her and her three sons. But, as she later put it, "God had a plan."

Lisa began coming to my Encouragers Sunday school class because it helped her see how many different ways God had blessed her in spite of her challenges. For the past fourteen years she had been a successful artist when marketing her products at local fine arts and crafts shows back in the Northeast. Because of her family situation she "could no longer devote two- and three-day weekends to sit and wait for the sale to come by." As she recovered from her broken leg, she worked from 9:00 a.m. to 5:00 p.m. every day on her art. Ultimately she decided it was time to take a leap of faith and see what God would do. She signed up for a renowned artists' trade show in New York City—a three-day event at the Jacob Javits Center in Manhattan. She had to take money from her savings to cover the enormous expenses but felt like the time was right to try to make her dreams come true.

She arrived in New York City on cloud nine. She knew God was with her and that He had not sent her to New York to return without some kind of blessing. She elected to have a positive attitude despite a remote corner booth assignment and told herself it would make it easy for contacts to find her in the cavernous exhibition hall.

Lisa had spent five months doing her homework. She had sent out over one hundred invitations to buyers to drop by her booth, sent fifty-one E-mails, and made more than twenty cold calls before the show. She knew the names of people who would be there buying. When people would breeze by her booth without so much as a glance in her direction, she'd greet them with, "How are you?" They would respond in kind, of course, and Lisa would reply, "I'm doing better than good!" That reply almost always caused the buyers to look up, walk over, and begin a conversation. They were intrigued by someone who said she was "doing better than good."

Even though Lisa said, "I'm doing better than good," it wasn't because she was selling tons of products. She really believed her life was "better than good." She'd made the trip to New York, was meeting people and making contacts and having a ball. Selling products was not the determining factor in the status of her life. Things were "better than good" before she got there, and she was convinced they'd be "better than good" when she got home.

As a result of her efforts, Lisa left New York with twenty-two companies interested in her products. She has since signed two contracts with New York Graphic Society Publishing Group to use her images on products they sell in stores across America as well as galleries and museums. She also has signed a licensing agreement with Encore Promotions, a division of Bradshaw International, to use her art images on a line of holiday dinnerware for the 2006 Christmas selling season.

Lisa really believes that adopting the optimistic attitude that life is "better than good" as she greeted her future customers in New York was instrumental in many of them responding positively to her. And so do I! People are attracted to optimism—they love to be around those who believe life is a string of good events tied together one after another.

I have to close Lisa's wonderful story with a disclaimer: I'm not suggesting that you should use the "better than good" phrase just to increase your business. Lisa didn't, and neither should you. You should use it because you believe in your heart that life is, indeed, "better than good." But with that kind of forward-looking perspective, I would be the last person to limit what God might do in your life. Give it a try and see what happens!

A "Better Than Good" Promotion

Kelly Green has worked for thirteen years at North Dallas Bank &

Trust Co., a company he loves working for. During that time he has received a number of promotions, including being made an assistant vice president in June 2000. But at the end of 2001 he was transferred to a different part of the bank that required him to prove himself all over again.

In April 2004, he began attending my Sunday school class and started using the "I'm doing better than good" response with everyone who asked how he was doing. And by the end of 2004 he had been promoted to vice president in his new department at the bank. When he received a performance evaluation from his supervisor, it contained this comment: "Cooperates very well with his supervisor, executives, and coworkers. His attitude is 'better than good'!"

Kelly got promoted because of his hard work. But he's told me that the simple "better than good" phrase has impacted how he approaches his work. He's confident that his supervisor and others were appreciative of his continually optimistic approach. I know if I had been his supervisor at the bank, I would have been. Who wouldn't be eager to promote an employee whose outlook on life is always "better than good"?

"Better Than Good" Food

When you drive through Texas, it's hard to miss one of the most popular food chains in the state: Luby's Cafeterias, where food "Tastes Like Texas, Feels Like Home." (No, I'm not paid to say that. Luby's 131 locations are an institution in Texas and four other regional states, so the saying is commonplace in our neck of the woods.)

The Redhead and I were eating one day at our local Luby's, which happens to be the busiest and most productive in the chain. Manager John Cartwright is terrific—upbeat, gung ho, and loved by his employees. But the day we went to eat, the outdoor marquee read, "People would die for our blackened tilapia." I called John over and said, "Nobody is going to die for a fish! Why don't you change the sign to read, 'Our blackened tilapia is better than good'?" He had changed the sign before we finished our meal!

Since then John's continued using the phrase on his marquee, and the word is spreading that the food and his employees are "better than good."

Sometimes, all it takes is a word, a phrase, or a thought planted in someone's mind to change his or her whole life. It truly pays to watch closely what and how you think. It is said that Frank Outlaw expressed the power of our thoughts this way:

Watch your thoughts; they become words.
Watch your words; they become actions.
Watch your actions; they become habits.
Watch your habits; they become character.
Watch your character; for it becomes your destiny!

You may have never connected your thoughts with your destiny before, but I hope you do from now on. And I hope you'll begin by thinking and believing that life is "better than good."

"Better Than Good" Books

Charles Osgood, the famed CBS wordsmith, once made this observation: compared to the spoken word, a picture is a pitiful thing indeed. We're used to saying that a picture is worth a thousand words, and maybe sometimes it is when you're trying to explain something unfamiliar to another person. But pictures simply do not have the ability to lodge themselves in the human heart like words do.

Take the Bible, for instance—the best-selling book in history, and it has no pictures! The Bible says that God's words are "living and active" and can find their way between "soul and spirit . . . able to judge the thoughts and intentions of the heart" (Hebrews

4:12). In another place the Bible says God's words never return to Him empty without accomplishing the purpose for which they were sent (see Isaiah 55:10–11).

The pen has always been mightier than the sword and can move people to action like nothing else. In my Sunday school class there was a young woman who was struggling with several critical issues in her life. She told me later how a few simple things I said in that class—"Failure is an event, not a person"; "Yesterday really did end last night"; "God not only permits U-turns in life, He encourages them"—opened up whole new vistas of possibility for her. Simple words, profound impact.

If words have that big an impact on our lives, why don't we work harder to fill our minds with the most profound words we can? The Bible says we ought to dwell on (think and meditate on) things that are true, honorable, right, pure, lovely, of good repute, excellent, and worthy of praise (see Philippians 4:8). And yet most of what we read is far from those standards. And think of the opportunities we have: audio books for the car, CDs, cassette tapes, podcasts for your iPod, not to mention plain old books. (Even in this age of techno gadgets, nothing has yet replaced a good book by a warm fire. And I don't think it ever will.)

Besides the Bible, I encourage people to consume one category of inspiring thoughts above all others: the biographies of great men and women. Andy Andrews is one of the most godly, inspiring men I've ever met. Reading biographies changed his life and the lives of thousands of other people.

Andy's mother died when he was nineteen, and his father was killed shortly thereafter in a car crash. He was homeless for a while and even considered suicide after a string of bad choices left him looking for a reason to live. He began spending a lot of time in the public library, where he read biographies, searching for clues as to what characterized successful people.

The result of more than two hundred biographies he read was

The Traveler's Gift: Seven Decisions That Determine Personal Success. He was turned down by fifty-one publishers (I think he decided perseverance was one of the characteristics of successful people!) before a publisher accepted his manuscript. His book stayed on the *New York Times'* best-seller list for seventeen weeks. He told the story of a fictional character traveling back in time and conversing with seven successful individuals about the meaning of life and how to find success.

Andy credits the reading of the Bible and those two hundred biographies with filling his mind with the seeds for accomplishment. Think what the world would have missed if he had chosen to fill his mind with less noble thoughts!

"Better Than Good" Thoughts

Think what the world might miss based on what you're filling your mind with. We pore over the newspaper every day like it has the secrets to life in it. Most people would say they aren't inspired to be a better person by reading the paper, yet they do it. They'd also say they are inspired to reach greater heights by reading the Bible and other great books—but they rarely do. Why do we spend more time reading what won't help us than reading what will?

I read the paper nearly every day because it provides information that helps me in my work (stories, facts, trends, and the like). But I don't read it at the expense of reading and studying my Bible. I read each daily so I know what both sides are up to!

I love the story of the Eskimo who used to pit his lead sled dogs against one another in weight-pulling contests. The old Eskimo had one black dog and one white dog, and they seemed to out-pull each other on a regular basis. Amazingly the old Eskimo always placed his bet on the winning dog. Long after the two dogs were retired, one of the villagers asked how he always knew which one of the two evenly matched dogs would win in a given contest. How did he know which one to bet on? "It's very easy," the old

Eskimo said. "I bet on the one I'd been feeding all week."

Dogs and minds are no different—the one we feed is the one that's going to win. If you feed the base, carnal mind, that's the one that's going to rule your life. But if you feed the spiritual mind, the mind that feeds on honorable and noble things, that's the mind that will rule. The mind is always hungry and will take in whatever we give it. We just need to give it the fare God intended for it to live on.

Two teen–aged brothers approached their father with a request to be allowed to see a certain popular movie. It had a few brief elements that gave it an R rating, but they felt those negatives were offset by the importance of the story and the quality of the actors. They begged their father to relax his standards just this once. And he promised he'd consider it.

The next night when the three of them sat down to discuss the movie, the father brought a plate of beautiful brownies to the table. "You know," he said, "that we only use the finest ingredients when we bake brownies—eggs, cocoa, flour, milk, and nuts. You can eat as many as you like, but I need to tell you that I relaxed my standards just a bit this time and included a little—not much— dog poop in the batter. But don't let that stop you. Help yourself."

You already know that those brownies went untouched.

I learned many years ago that it was virtually impossible for me to inspire other people to fill their minds with positive, honorable, and successful thinking if I wasn't doing the same thing myself. My objective is to lift people up, not drag them down. Therefore, I have to continually be moving to higher ground myself. And I can't do that if I'm filling my mind with the standard American mental diet of nonedifying thoughts. I work hard at protecting myself from things that I don't want to be in my mind. My eye-gate and ear-gate are under constant surveillance when it comes to television, movies, the Internet, music, conversations, and reading material.

I have heard more than one heartbreaking story from men who have struggled with pornography since their teenage years because they took a "quick look" and got hooked. Marriages and families have been ruined because of allowing unholy images and words to dominate the mind. I was shocked and disappointed a few years ago when two popular newspaper advice columnists encouraged couples whose marriages were no longer exciting to get a boost by viewing pornography together. That's bad advice. You cannot dump garbage into a well and expect the water to be good. You cannot feed the mind on demoralizing filth and expect your life to be good, clean, pure, powerful, and motivated.

"Better Than Good" Change of Mind

The first two and one-half years I was in sales I really struggled. Then I attended a meeting conducted by P. C. Merrell. He apparently saw something in me, because after the meeting he told me he had been watching me for months and thought I could be the national leader in sales—in a company with over seven thousand sales reps! He said he thought I could be one of the great ones—even an executive in the company—if I would only apply myself.

I previously saw myself as a small-time, small-town guy with little potential. But he painted a different verbal picture that changed my self-image immediately. And that year I finished number two in the nation! Don't misunderstand. Up to that time I had learned all the techniques of sales—the salesperson was trained but the person himself was not. But P. C. Merrell's words changed my mind—and my life.

This final, fabulous story is about a woman who was a beloved associate in my own company—a person who blossomed in ways I've rarely seen equaled. When Melissa Hovendick came to work for us, I honestly wondered whether she could be successful in her job. When she was transferred to sales, I was blown away. Within months, she was our number one salesperson. Here's Melissa's explanation: "You can change where you are and what you are by changing what goes in your mind. I am living proof."

Melissa's story is so incredible I could write a book on it alone; but let me give you some highlights. She was raised in an abusive, alcoholic home; had suicidal thoughts at age twelve; married an abusive husband at age eighteen to escape the abusive situation at home; and was constantly sick due to emotional stress. Melissa was employed as a hair dresser and had never worked in an office when she responded to an ad for a filing job at the Zig Ziglar Corporation and was chosen over other more-qualified candidates.

From the time she arrived, Melissa embraced our philosophy on how to have a "better than good" life. She began to saturate her mind with the right things. She listened to our recordings, and recordings of the New Testament "nonstop!" She even switched to Christian radio. Melissa went from being in the doctor's office almost weekly to working out regularly and feeding her body the right foods and nutritional supplements. She also began to go to night school to improve her education. She quit watching television shows that were not constructive and reading magazines that caused her to feel bad about herself. She prayed constantly, quit seeing people who were not a positive influence, and instead surrounded herself with people she admired and respected. Melissa guarded her mind and allowed only positive input; eventually she left her abusive husband.

Melissa began a steady round of promotions in our company. In every department, one of the women would reach out to her and, seeing her potential, encourage her. She went from filing to customer service to data processing to sales in quick succession. She started at our company making $17,000 a year but became the company's top salesperson and record setter.

Melissa's mentor in sales introduced her to a friend in Omaha, Nebraska, named John, who was a nice, young man but not a Christian. She invited him to one of our seminars, where he became a

Christian, started using my principles, and experienced a dramatic change in his own life. Melissa was eventually offered a job in Omaha by a Ziglar Training Systems client. She accepted, moved to Omaha, and married John Hovendick. She continued to listen to our teaching tapes and Scripture to, as she puts it, "replace all the old tapes in my mind with new ones" (see Romans 12:2).

Eight years ago Melissa was hired by another company to improve the company so it could be sold. A year later that company sold and her bosses asked her to stay on to help them start a brand-new business. Starting with only a handful of brochures, she hit the road selling and grew that company from zero to fifty million dollars in annual revenue. She's been the VP of sales at that company for five years, and it is now the largest privately owned company in her industry's very narrow market segment. Her salary grew from sixty-five thousand dollars to six figures annually (and the first number was not a one).

She and John have a wonderful marriage, two beautiful children, and a home on five acres of land. John owns his own tree care company and Melissa continues to work as VP of sales for her company on a part-time basis (and still pulls down six figures part-time). She still practices the habits that caused her life to change: "I have continued to make the choice to constantly watch what I am putting in my mind, because I know the choices you make today will affect you the rest of your life—for the positive or the negative."

Dear reading friend, if you run into Melissa Hovendick somewhere today and ask her how her life is, I know she will tell you it is "better than good." Wouldn't you agree?

And I believe your life will be "better than good" as well if you will do what Melissa did, and what the title of this chapter suggests: watch what you feed your mind.

5 | Perception and Attitude

The essence of optimism is that it takes no account of the present, but it is a source of inspiration, of vitality and hope where others have resigned; it enables a man to hold his head high, to claim the future for himself and not to abandon it to his enemy.

DIETRICH BONHOEFFER

A pessimist is someone who complains about the noise when opportunity knocks.

MICHAEL LEVINE

The greatest discovery of my generation is that a human being can alter his life by altering his attitudes of mind.

WILLIAM JAMES

Compare what you want with what you have, and you'll be unhappy; compare what you deserve with what you have, and you'll be happy.

EVAN ESAR

Optimism is an intellectual choice.

DIANA SCHNEIDER

Human felicity is produced not so much by great pieces of good fortune that seldom happen as by little advantages that occur every day.

BENJAMIN FRANKLIN

S teve Fossett is a passionate man. An investment banker by trade, his passion is not money; it's adventure: altitude, speed, endurance, and danger. He has swum the English Channel, competed in the Alaskan Iditarod, and raced the twenty-four-hour Le Mans auto race. But what Steve Fossett is best known for is his around-the-world hot air balloon attempts—and achievement. In July 2002, his sixth attempt was successful. He became the first person to circumnavigate the globe in a hot air balloon.

On one of his previous attempts, in January 1997, Fossett left St. Louis, Missouri, and made it as far as India before having to land his balloon. It's a description of an incident on that trip, reported in *National Geographic* magazine, that I want to call to your attention.

Heading east across the Atlantic Ocean, the prevailing winds were carrying him at 24,500 feet, straight for the northern African country of Libya. And this was a problem. Libya had refused to grant him permission to fly in its air space, meaning they could shoot him down if they so desired. Since hot air balloons are subject to the prevailing winds, he had no way to turn and avoid Libyan air space.

The only way hot air balloons can turn is by adjusting their altitude. They can release helium out of the balloon and drop to a lower altitude and, it is hoped, pick up a crosswind. Or they can heat the balloon and ascend to a higher altitude for the same purpose.

So Fossett vented helium from the balloon, descended sixty-three hundred feet, and caught an air current blowing southeast that allowed him to skirt the southern border of Libya. When it was safe, he heated the balloon, rose ten thousand feet, and caught a wind blowing due east that put him back on course. Though he had to set down in India, he still set records on that trip for the longest distance and duration in a manned balloon flight.

Another world-class balloonist, Bertrand Piccard, commenting on Fossett's altitude strategy, made this insightful comment: "In the balloon, you are prisoners of the wind, and you go only in the direction of the wind. In life people think they are prisoners of circumstance. But in the balloon, as in life, you can change altitude, and when you change altitude, you change direction. You are not a prisoner anymore."

Bertrand Piccard hit the nail on the head: "When you change altitude, you change direction. You are not a prisoner anymore." For our purposes in this chapter, I'm going to beg Mr. Piccard's indulgence and change his word from "altitude" to "attitude": "When you change attitude, you change direction. You are not a prisoner anymore." Attitude is to life what altitude is to hot air ballooning—a way to remain free from disturbances that have the potential to send us crashing to the ground below.

If you are among the people in this life who feel like they are prisoners to the prevailing winds of circumstance, I have news for you. By adjusting your attitude, you can rise above that which seems inevitable and choose your destination instead of being taken where the winds of change dictate.

A Matter of Perspective

You may remember the torturous career of American speed skater Dan Jansen. In his bid to win an Olympic gold medal, he suffered setbacks in 1984, 1988, and 1992. In his book *Full Circle*, he tells about how he learned to keep disappointments in perspective.

When he was nine years old, Jansen was competing in a youth national speed skating championship in Minnesota. Coming around a turn on his way to victory his skate caught a lane marker and he fell. As a result, he lost the championship by one point. He started crying and had not stopped six hours later when the family pulled into the driveway of their home. His father hadn't said a word about his loss all the way home. But as they got out of the car, with Dan still crying over his loss, his father said quietly, "You know, Dan, there's more to life than skating around in a circle."

If you think that father was being less than sympathetic with his heartbroken son, think again. What he did was put that defeat in perspective. Sure, it's great to win at anything or everything. But the greatest races in life are not those where we run, skate, sprint, throw, or sell more than the next guy. Those are circumstances—some wins, some losses—that serve as mile markers to tell us how we're progressing in the real race: that of developing the kind of character that will produce the "better than good" life.

It's a mistaken notion to believe that happy people are those who experience one success or victory after another while unhappy people experience just the opposite. Research shows that happy people and unhappy people tend to have very similar experiences in life. The difference is perspective: unhappy people spend more time thinking about life's unpleasant events; they become introspective and self-centered in their thinking, and thus in their living. Happy people, on the other hand, take life's events in stride. They have a positive worldview that allows room for disappointments and failures along the way. They seek out and depend upon facts that bolster their perspective on life; they are outward focused and centered on others.

Knowing whether someone has recently suffered a personal tragedy or personal success is not a good predictor of how satisfied he is with his life. People who have experienced similar life events can wind up with nearly opposite responses. Take job promotions, for instance. Did you know not everyone is happy when promoted in his or her job or career? Sounds strange, but it's true. Positive-thinking people are excited when they get a promotion because it means new challenges, responsibilities, and opportunities—not to mention more financial rewards. But people who don't have a positive perspective, while loving the increase in salary, groan at the likelihood of new responsibilities and challenges. They think it's going to be longer hours, later nights, and a disruption to a lifestyle with which they had grown comfortable. In a group of people, the same event will reveal a difference in perspectives on life.

When something disappointing happens to people with a positive perspective on life, they view it as an exception to the rule. For those people, the rule is that life is good—it's a great adventure full of possibility and reward. So when a setback occurs, they view it as an exception that proves the rule: "See, the fact that this rare downturn has occurred proves that, the vast majority of the time, life is good!"

But when that same reversal happens to people with a negative perspective on life, they view it as confirming what they already believed: life is basically a disappointing experience, a string of defeats interrupted only by the rare glimpse of victory. They believe those events confirm that they are losers, destined to stub their toe with every step they take.

To put it another way, positive people don't react to life; they respond. Responding is positive; reacting is negative. Think of the word *reactionary*. What image does it bring to mind? It's someone with his heels dug in, someone in a defensive posture, someone who strikes back. But a responder is one who engages, one who takes the offense, someone who reaches out rather than striking back.

Responders don't have their heads in the sand, living in denial. They recognize the seriousness of some of life's events, but they see them as things that simply alter their course, not close it down. Everyone knows that life is not lived in a straight line from womb to tomb. Life is a series of adjustments, always keeping the goal in view. Something negative happens? Fine, we'll respond by believing there is a divine purpose for that event and adjust our plans accordingly. For the Christian responder, Romans 8:28 is a life verse: "And we know that God causes all things to work together for good to those who love God, to those who are called according to His purpose."

It would be easy for anyone to read that verse and say, "I

believe that. I believe that whatever happens in life is what is supposed to happen. Like the song says, '*Qué será, será.*'" Others take a fatalistic approach to life and say, "Hey, why fight city hall? I'm just one person on the beach trying to stay out of the way of the incoming tide of the universe. It's bigger than me, man, and I'm just going with the flow."

Actually, neither of those views are consistent with the verse I quoted. Why? Because for the Christian, life has nothing to do with chance or fatalism. God orchestrates all the events in our lives to achieve the goal of growing us up before we grow old. Life is not a pinball machine where we are the little steel ball being flipped from pillar to post. Rather, if we know God, the events in our life are coming to us through the filter of His purposes—even the disappointing things that are often a result of our own bad choices.

I hope you have an eternal perspective that allows you to see everything that happens in your life from God's point of view.

Eternal Optimists

The March 1988 issue of *Rotarian* magazine told about a wild-life organization that was offering a five-thousand-dollar bounty for every wolf that was captured alive for purposes of relocation. Sam and Jed took up the challenge and became bounty/fortune hunters. Sam was especially confident, given his and Jed's knowledge of the wolf's habitat, that they could make a mint.

They spent every day and night scouring the territory looking for wolf packs to target, but didn't make a single sighting. Exhausted after days of searching, they fell asleep late one night around their campfire. Something caused Sam to wake up out of his deep sleep. Leaning up on one elbow, he discovered that he and Jed were surrounded by about fifty growling wolves with flaming eyes and bared teeth. He poked Jed with a stick and whispered, "Jed! Wake up! We're rich!"

That, my friend, is a textbook example of optimism. Don't you just love optimists? They're the ones who spend their last twenty dollars on a cash box to hold their future earnings. They're the ones who go after Moby Dick in a rowboat and take a five-gallon bucket of tartar sauce with them. Optimists are the ones we love to be around because of their energy and the sense of possibility they see in every situation.

Optimists are full of passion. They believe they're on this earth for a purpose and have no intention of stopping until that purpose is fulfilled. Their attitudes are positive, their perspectives eternal, and their enthusiasm contagious. They have a glow that fills the darkest of hours with light. It's a proverbial saying, but optimists truly believe it: there is a silver lining in every cloud.

Optimists expect a favorable outcome! I love what Lawrence Fargher said about the optimist: "Our American way of life is so full of blessings that no man can count them all, but the greatest of them all is the optimist." There is a mellow radiance about the optimist that impacts social and business ventures in a way that technology and brilliance never can. Optimists are the hand that grasps the tools of possibility and puts them to work when everyone else has called it a day. The optimist carries an atmosphere of hope and encouragement that becomes infectious. His associates lose their gloom in the light of his "can-do-ism."

Because optimists are not the kind of people who talk about their troubles to others, some people think they're disingenuous. Not so! Optimists aren't in denial about anything. In fact, they're the most realistic people you'll ever meet because they call a spade a spade in every case. They're honest. They're the ones who say, "Okay, this is something we weren't expecting. Our largest customer is not renewing his contract. But at least our inventory problems are solved, because our biggest supplier just went out of business! Now, those are the facts. Let's see what opportunities this new situation offers us."

Optimists love facts because they are like the pieces of life's jigsaw puzzle—you need them all to put the puzzle together. Optimists will lay all the facts on the table, not for the purpose of saying, "Woe is me," but in order to start putting together the strategy for the next day, week, month, and year.

When you get right down to it, optimists are happy people. At least, that's been my experience. My trusty 1828 Noah Webster dictionary says *happiness* is "the agreeable sensations which spring from the enjoyment of good; that state of being in which desires are gratified; the enjoyment of pleasure without pain." I think happiness is what an optimist experiences when his expected favorable outcome has come to pass.

Optimists really believe the goal they are working toward is going to come to pass in one form or another. They are like a craftsman who patiently toils away in his shop, bringing an object of beauty to light. They are like a child building a sand castle on a beach. They are like a parent making it through the teenage years with a child who has lost his way, knowing he will find it in time. They are like a person who is content in the life she is living, believing there is deep meaning in the simplest of achievements and the briefest of encounters with others.

I hope you are an optimist, my friend. Not everyone is, but everyone should be. I will tell you that if you want to have passion in life, you can't be a pessimist. Pessimism will drain the passion out of you like oil out of a crankcase. Just try getting a life in gear that is missing the oil of passion and see how far you get.

Gratitude Attitude

There's another way that an eternal perspective manifests itself—and that is in gratitude.

In Texas, retired Hall of Fame baseball pitcher Nolan Ryan carries iconic status. Not only is he one of the greatest pitchers of all time, he's a humble family man and businessman who wins praise from the homefolk for his down-to-earth ways. Ruth Ryan,

Nolan's wife, related an anecdote in her book, *Covering Home*, that says a lot about gratitude:

> It probably happened the first time on the high school baseball diamond in Alvin, Texas, in the mid-1960s. Then it happened repeatedly for three decades after that. Inevitably, sometime during a game, Nolan would pop up out of the dugout and scan the stands behind home plate, looking for me. He would find my face and grin at me, maybe snapping his head up in a quick nod as if to say, "There you are; I'm glad." I'd wave and flash him a smile. Then he'd duck under the roof and turn back to the game.
>
> It was a simple moment, never noted in record books or career summaries. But of all the moments in all the games, it was the one most important to me.

I can imagine that the wives of some wealthy superstars might be most grateful for the fancy cars, the palatial homes, or the jewels and bangles their husbands provided. But I am struck with Ruth Ryan's account because it shows the reality of gratitude in the smallest things in life. For a wife to meet the searching eyes of her husband and receive a look and a grin that says, "I need you and I'm glad you're here"—that's a powerful statement. It would be easy for the wife of a professional athlete to resent her husband's travel schedule or get tired of attending home games. But gratitude at the idea of being loved and needed was enough to keep Ruth Ryan "covering home" for decades.

The Practicality of Gratitude

It is more than a cliché to say that the more you express gratitude for what you have, the more you will have to express gratitude for. It's also true, according to Christian psychiatrist Frank Minirth, the more you complain about the problems you have, the more problems you'll have to complain about.

Whatever happened to children learning to say thank you? It's so rare today that we're almost surprised when we hear anyone say it. The "entitlement" age in which we live has caused a lot of people to think, "I'm entitled. . . . I'm owed. . . . I'm due. . . ." But is that really true? Not at all. People who lose their sense of gratitude—or never had one—are people who will live with a chip on their shoulder all their lives. Spending all their time trying to collect what's "rightfully" theirs, they'll never get around to living a life of passion.

Some people just don't get the gratitude thing. Like the farmer who woke up in the hospital to find his loyal wife by his side, ready to comfort him. He said, "You know, Martha, when we first married, hail destroyed our first crop and you were there by my side. Two years later, lightning struck our barn and destroyed the crop and barn, and you were there by my side. Still later, when we got into dairy farming, a disease ravaged the whole herd and you were right there by my side. Through it all, Martha, you were always there by my side."

She responded, "Yes, George, I was."

He said, "Now that I'm really sick here in the hospital, here you are again by my side."

She said, "Yes, I am, George."

Then George responded, "You know, Martha, I'm beginning to believe you're a jinx!"

Some people just don't know how good they've got it. I read about a little three-year-old girl in France, Marie Thielle, who won a bronze medal for her act of courage. When her two-year-old playmate, Dennis, fell into a swimming pool, she reached over the edge of the pool, grabbed his hair, and pulled him to the surface, saving his life. Everyone, especially Dennis's parents, was so grateful for Marie's bravery and quick action. Well, almost everyone. "Dennis doesn't like me now," Marie later reported, "because it hurt when I pulled his hair."

There are people today who, instead of being thankful for the medicine that will make them better, complain about the taste. But not passionate people who have an attitude of gratitude. They see everything in life as being a gift from the hand of a good and loving God. They take nothing for granted and give thanks for everything—like a grin and nod from a hundred feet away in a baseball stadium.

People make a mistake thinking they have to be happy to be grateful, and that to be happy they have to experience positive "happenings" in their life. Wrong. Happiness doesn't emanate from good happenings—it springs from something deeper called *joy*, regardless of what happens. Joy is that deep-rooted sense that the keys to success in life are hung behind the curtain that separates heaven from earth. Joy comes from knowing that "God has a plan and I'm part of it." One of the letters in the New Testament is called "the epistle of joy." Guess where the author, Paul the apostle, was when he wrote it: in prison! Need I say more? If you can have joy in prison, you can have it when you run out of gas, get fired, have a best friend desert you, or get sick.

Some people look at me strangely when I say this, but I experienced the deep joy that comes only from God even in the darkest days of grieving after our beloved daughter, Suzan, died. My tears could not wash away my passion for life, because it is rooted in gratitude for a God who has a plan for my life. Instead of being angry that Suzan was taken from us, I am grateful for the time we had with her.

Grateful people are happy people, but the happiest people are those who have the joy that comes only as a result of an intimate relationship with God.

Attitude Is Attitude

I can't emphasize enough the impact of attitude on the journey toward peak performance. Attitude is a mental outlook—a frame of mind. It's how you think based on what you know to be true. It's a reflection of your faith, a sign of your confidence that life is not about you, nor even about your happiness or success. It is about God and His plan for your life.

I want to be absolutely clear before I close this chapter: I am not speaking about a contrived, manufactured, positive attitude that is assumed to impress or even manipulate others, including yourself. The attitude I'm talking about cannot be conjured up at a moment's notice. It is what you are filled with, what instantaneously spills out when you are bumped in the process of going through this life. It is an integral part of who you are.

If you have a bad attitude, you have to have an internal change of heart to get a good one. Don't worry—you don't have to operate on yourself. God is the heart surgeon who can give you a new heart. He doesn't repair old hearts; He replaces them with brand-new ones, filled with love, joy, peace, patience, kindness, goodness, faithfulness, gentleness, and self-control (see Galatians 5:22–23). If you had all those qualities in your life, your attitude would be the perfect place for passion to be born and stay alive, leading you to the peak performance you were created to reach.

And it will be an attitude that is genuine, winsome, humble, and engaging—not something you have to pump up every morning like the hot air balloons of Steve Fossett. In your life and mine, friend, attitude is altitude. It's all we need to stay above the fray going on beneath.

Check your perspective. Check your attitude. By this point in the book I hope I've whetted your passion's appetite for the "better than good" life. Because now it's time to start letting passion do what it is supposed to do: be the fuel that propels us to peak performance! I'll meet you in Part II: The Peak Performance of the "Better Than Good" Life.

PART II:

THE PEAK PERFORMANCE OF THE "BETTER THAN GOOD" LIFE

6 | Develop a Passionate Plan

Plan ahead—it wasn't raining when Noah built the ark.
RICHARD CUSHING

As a prominent educator has expressed it, Americans generally spend so much time on things that are urgent that we have none left to spend on those that are important.
GUSTAV METZMAN

Make your plans as fantastic as you like, because twenty-five years from now, they will seem mediocre. Make your plans ten times as great as you first planned, and twenty-five years from now you will wonder why you did not make them fifty times as great.
HENRY CURTIS

You and I must not complain if our plans break down if we have done our part. That probably means that the plans of One who knows more than we do have succeeded.
EDWARD E. HALE

We can't cross a bridge until we come to it; but I always like to lay down a pontoon ahead of time.
BERNARD M. BARUCH

Planning is bringing the future into the present so you can do something about it now.
ALAN LAKEIN

In the September 1992 issue of his organization's newsletter, Dr. James Dobson shared an anecdote that illustrates a tension in life we all have to live with:

The famous architect Frank Lloyd Wright once told of an incident that would have seemed insignificant to the casual observer, but which had a profound influence on the rest of his life. The winter when he was nine years old, young Frank went walking across a snow-covered field with his reserved, no-nonsense uncle. As the two of them reached the far end of the field, his uncle stopped and turned around. He pointed to his own tracks in the snow, as straight and true as an arrow's flight from one end of the field to the other. Then he pointed out young Frank's tracks meandering all over the field. "Notice how your tracks wander aimlessly from the fence to the cattle to the woods and back again," his uncle said. "And see how my tracks aim directly to my goal. There is an important lesson in that."

Years later, when Frank was a world-famous architect, he liked to tell how that experience had greatly contributed to his philosophy in life: "I determined right then," he'd say with a twinkle in his eye, "not to miss most things in life, as my uncle had."

So who was the wiser of the two? Was it the uncle who focused on his objective and let nothing take him off course? Or was it young Frank, who took the creative and impulsive approach, focusing more on the journey than the destination?

The answer is yes—they were both right! The uncle was focused on a goal and was committed to letting nothing get him off track. He knew the shortest distance between where he was and where he wanted to be was a straight line. Young Frank, on the other hand, loved the journey. He was willing to delay getting to the end of the field as long as possible in order to experience everything along the way. In fact, he might never have made it to the end of the field had he not been keeping up with his uncle.

There is a tension in life we all wrestle with: how to find the middle ground, or balance, between the rigid pursuit of goals and remaining flexible at the same time. How do we know when it's right to delay reaching the goal, or perhaps choose an entirely different destination, in order to take advantage of opportunities we didn't foresee when we began the journey?

In this chapter we're going to talk about passionate planning. There's no sense in having passion in life if you don't apply it. That's like filling up the tank of your car with the highest octane gas and then not going anywhere. The whole concept of true *peak performance* implies that there is something you want to do, somewhere you want to go with your life. And that suggests the need for knowing how to plan—and how to remain flexible enough to adjust your plan as the need arises.

Life Is a Journey

All the truly successful people I have met in my life—and by successful, I don't mean successful in this world's eyes—believe success is a process, that life is a journey. They don't believe success is defined by material wealth, climbing one certain mountain or finally walking through one particular door. Rather, they believe success is a way of living that brings glory to God and contentment and peace to themselves.

When it comes to planning, they submit all their plans to God and ask Him to guide their steps. The wisest man who ever lived, King Solomon, penned proverbs that support this notion of success. Here they are in the popular modern translation *The Message:*

- *"Mortals make elaborate plans, but GOD has the last word"* (Proverbs 16:1).
- *"Put GOD in charge of your work, then what you've planned will take place"* (Proverbs 16:3).
- *"We plan the way we want to live, but only GOD makes us able to live it"* (Proverbs 16:9).

The Ziglar summary of these verses is this: "Make your plans—but don't forget Who's really in charge." Here's another passage from the Bible that illustrates this principle from a practical perspective:

> *Come now, you who say, "Today or tomorrow we will go to such and such a city, and spend a year there and engage in business and make a profit." Yet you do not know what your life will be like tomorrow. You are just a vapor that appears for a little while and then vanishes away. Instead, you ought to say, "If the Lord wills, we will live and also do this or that." But as it is, you boast in your arrogance; all such boasting is evil. (James 4:13–16)*

The moment we become so arrogant that we think our plans are infallible, that's the moment our performance is likely to start a downward trend from "peak" to "poor." Someone once said, "If you want to hear God laugh, tell Him your plans." God doesn't laugh to make fun of us. He laughs because He knows what the future holds and we don't. If we could see the future as well as He does we'd probably laugh too.

Successful people—those whose performance remains at its peak—are those who have learned to keep their eye on the ball while remaining flexible at all times. They are willing to stay flexible and change their plans because they believe, having submitted their plans to God, that He is directing their steps.

Don't Postpone the Trip

I have met some people who are full of good intentions. There are a million things in life they want to do, but they just never get around to doing them. Some of that is due to laziness, but I believe the majority is due to fear—the fear of failure, the fear of not planning well enough to cover every contingency along the way, the fear that when they arrive the destination may look different than they hoped it would when they began. As a result, they postpone the journey all their lives because they can never plan thoroughly enough to remove all contingencies.

The best vacations our family ever took when our children were growing up were those that had a general goal and direction —say, going to California to enjoy Disneyland—but that allowed room for side trips, excursions, breakdowns, and delays. What if, between Texas and California, we decided to peel off and spend a day at the Grand Canyon? And what if we left Disneyland a day early in order to go to San Diego to visit the world-famous zoo in that city? We could either sit at home and never begin our trip because we were afraid our plan might get changed, or we could establish our goal and pack enough clothes and other resources to allow for diversions along the way.

Joe Sabah has written, "You don't have to be great to start. But you do have to start to be great." Right on! Too many people want to wait until everything is perfect—all possible contingencies are removed—before beginning. Even in the most critical activities of life (for example, brain surgery and space flight), contingencies are part of the process. Doctors don't know with 100 percent accuracy what they'll find when they operate. And NASA engineers, as history has tragically shown us, aren't certain that everything will go as planned on space flights. But they don't let those unknowns keep them from starting.

There is one sure way in life I know of to never reach your peak performance, and that is never to start!

When the Old Testament psalmist said, "Thy word is a lamp to my feet, and a light to my path" (Psalm 119:105), you have to remember what that meant in his day. Lamps were small clay objects filled with oil and a wick that produced light equivalent to that of a modern candle. How much of your path do you think such a lamp would illuminate? Just about enough to enable you to take one more step on a dark night.

We want a million-candle-power searchlight to illuminate our path. But where's the faith in that approach? If you could see every single bend in the road ahead and know what was around each one, how interesting would the trip be? You'd know everything that was going to happen before you started. And you wouldn't need a bit of creativity, resourcefulness, or courage.

People pursuing the "better than good" life know life is a journey, not a destination. They don't have to see the whole trip illuminated before they begin. They just need to see enough to take the first step, and the next, and the next. . . .

Don't Measure the Journey

You're going to read later in this book about Charles Goodyear, the man who discovered the process for making rubber into a product suitable for commercial applications. The problem is he died before ever seeing his discovery recognized and utilized. However, it was what he discovered in a decades-long journey that allows you and me to drive on rubber tires today.

If we make the destination more important than the journey, we'll either never begin for fear of not reaching it or find ourselves heartbroken at the end of life that we came close but never got there. I've already told you about George Washington Carver. His journey was to discover the secrets of nature. He would have been just as satisfied if, by the end of his life, he had created three products from the peanut instead of three hundred. That's because his plan was to begin a journey, not end a journey.

Think about Noah in the Old Testament. He didn't set out to become a ship builder. In fact, God's plan probably seemed a little far-fetched to Noah. It had never rained, so nobody knew what a flood was, and the flood wasn't supposed to happen for 120 years. That's what we'd call *long-range planning* today. But that didn't deter Noah. He began immediately, and when the flood came, he and his family were saved.

Sometimes it makes sense to dive in with nothing but passion and raw drive and begin the journey. Since life is about the journey, not the destination, the fulfillment is going to come along the way. Whether you've reached your anticipated destination at the end of the journey is almost irrelevant. The contribution you make along the way is what's important. You may pass the baton to others who take it across the finish line. You'll be remembered for your passion, persistence, and productivity regardless.

Don't you imagine that Noah faced some naysayers while building the ark? Again, remember it had never rained. The idea of water falling down from the sky and covering all the land would have seemed preposterous to Noah's friends. But he kept on. And so must you. If you listen to the naysayers—"You can't get there from here!"—you may never put your plan in motion.

Another reason not to measure your journey is because we all move at different speeds. (The cheetahs and the snails both made it to the ark in time.) And some plans take longer than others to bring to fruition. The point is to begin the journey and let it unfold in the amount of time you have and at the pace God designed you to move. If the path you're following is God's path for your life, you won't be late or early but will accomplish exactly what He intended.

And don't wait to become an expert before you begin. If you know enough to get through an eight-hour day on your journey, then you know enough to begin. You'll learn some things in that first eight hours that will give you something to work on tomorrow. Remember: if you haven't gone as far as the light you have will take you, then you don't need to complain about not having enough light to finish. We become experts the same way we become "better than good"—by having faith, taking action, learning as we go, and steadily, purposefully moving forward with hopeful expectations.

Passionate Planning

When you combine passion with planning, good things happen! In fact, there are seven benefits I want you to note:

1. YOU WILL STAY FOCUSED ON GOD

I know this is an assumption on my part—that you believe in God and are committing your plans to Him. It's so fundamental to the way I live my life that I put it at the top of my list and encourage you to make it number one on yours as well.

You see, planning requires a look into the future. And at best, on a clear day, I can see about a half mile, which isn't going to take me very far. I don't have a crystal ball, so how am I going to plan into the future when I can't see what's going to happen? I have to trust in God. I'm a simple man, not a rocket scientist, and I need answers that work. Committing my plans to God helps me keep Him at the forefront of my life as He and I partner together to live a "better than good" life.

2. YOU WILL LIVE WITHOUT FEAR

This obviously follows from the previous point. Fear is all about the future—not knowing what it will bring. If I trust my future to God, who does know what it will bring, and I believe God is good (which He is), then I have no reason to fear the future. If my plans are derailed or changed, I know God has a reason for that. I would rather have changed plans with God's blessing than fulfilled plans without His blessing.

3. YOU WILL BE INSPIRED

Inspiration is stimulation, and passionate planning results in your becoming energized to achieve your goals. Remember: passion in you is like fuel in your car. The "better than good" life cannot be lived without passion, nor can peak performance be obtained apart from it. That's why it is so incredibly important for you to discover your passion in this life.

4. YOU WILL WORK HARD

I am all for balance in this life over the long haul. You need to eat right and get plenty of sleep. But there are going to be times when you have to burn the candle at both ends to make your dreams come true. If you are averse to hard work, I don't think you'll ever live the "better than good" life. When you have passion and have a plan for implementing it, you will work hard to make that plan become a reality. I've discovered over the years that no success feels as good as the one achieved by hard work. In fact, there seems to be a corollary: the harder I work implementing a plan, the sweeter the success when it is realized.

5. YOU WILL WELCOME FAILURE AS PART OF YOUR EDUCATION

We've all heard the stories about Thomas Edison and the light-bulb, how he failed a thousand times before finding a filament that would work. He imported materials from all over the world trying to make a filament that wouldn't burn up. When one failed to work, he just crossed that material off his list and went on to the next one. I can just see him growing more and more excited with each failure, knowing he was that much closer to what would eventually work. It is said that when his laboratory caught fire and created a roaring inferno, he sent one of his assistants to get his wife: "Tell her to hurry! She'll never see such a fire as this!" Edison even got excited when his laboratory burned down!

It was Edison himself who said, "Many of life's failures are people who did not realize how close they were to success when they gave up."

6. YOU WILL KEEP HOPE ALIVE

It was Winston Churchill's passion for his homeland that kept the hope of his nation alive when London was bombed by the Germans. As frightened citizens huddled in basements and subways for safety, they would listen to Churchill's voice on the radio encouraging them not to lose hope—making them believe they would be victorious if they would not give up. Their city was nearly ruined, but it was not defeated.

The degree of hope you manifest by persevering through obstacles becomes a measure of your passion. When you make your plans, plan on discouragements and failures and obstacles, for you will have them. At the same time, plan on not giving up.

7. YOU WILL REACH YOUR GOD-GIVEN POTENTIAL

When we talk about the "better than good" life, we're talking about the life God created you to live. You know by now that I believe God created you to live a life you may have only dreamed about. It is filled with unlimited potential! When you commit your plans to Him and are filled with passion that only He can give, peak performance is what you should expect—and what you will receive. We're not talking about making a million dollars or becoming president of the United States (though that could happen). We're talking about your knowing in your heart of hearts that you are doing what you are supposed to be doing. You're happy, other people are blessed, and God is honored. That's reaching your God-given potential and living the "better than good" life.

Dynamics of Strategic Planning

I'm calling the following four points "dynamics" instead of "steps," because they are bigger than steps; they permeate the planning process from beginning to end. There is never a time in the execution of your plans—from dream to destination—that you will not experience all four of these dynamics:

1. HAVE FAITH

For me, that means faith in God through Jesus Christ. For you, it might boil down to confidence. But you are going to have to have it in the planning stages, the execution stage, the obstacle stage, the reversal stage, and in the give-up-the-ship stage.

2. TAKE ACTION

The moment you stop taking action, everything in your plan stops. Even mental reflection is action. Prayer is action. Seeking advice is action. Taking a weekend of R and R is action. Make sure something is happening all the time toward the accomplishment of your plan.

3. LEARN AS YOU GO

The bottom line here is to learn from your mistakes and failures. There has never been a perfect human plan and never will be. Edison's lightbulb was a great start, but it continues to be refined today. Life is a classroom—only those who are willing to be life-long learners will move to the head of the class.

Nucor Steel is an example of a company that succeeded when most other American steel companies failed. They learned how to make steel in a new kind of plant situated in new parts of the country using new kinds of workers. They broke the century-old mold for how to make steel by thinking outside the box when cheaper foreign steel drove other American companies out of business. They charted a new path—did something that had never been done in their industry—and survived and succeeded. Those who learn, prosper.

4. PERSEVERE WITH HOPE

If you aren't willing to fight for your plan from start to finish, there is reason to wonder if it ever should have been launched. If you want to see this (and the other three) dynamic in action over a period of years, read the story of Abraham and Sarah in the Old Testament. God promised Abraham he would become the father of a people as numerous as the sand on the seashore. But he had no child, and he and Sarah were ninety-nine and ninety years of age, respectively. But they had a son, whom God then told Abraham to kill as a sacrifice—which would have ended the plan. The fact that the Jewish nation exists today means the plan succeeded. (I'll let you read the story in Genesis 12–22 and Hebrews 11:8–19 to see how.)

It doesn't matter what your plan is—to lose weight, stop smoking, start a business or a ministry, go back to school—you will need to keep these four dynamics alive throughout the process. And if you do, you will succeed.

Real-Life Planning

Linda Burzynski's husband attended one of my company's seminars in Dallas, and she got a new husband in return. She was so amazed at the number of changes she saw Victor making in his life that she decided to make some changes of her own. She was expecting her first baby and wanted to become the best person and mother she could be. By studying the material Victor brought home from the seminar, she discovered a level of potential she had never realized before in her own life. It was truly an "Aha!" experience for her.

Suddenly, she was experiencing (1) *new faith.* She began to (2) *take action* and says to this day she is (3) *still learning.* The changes she has experienced have given her the ability to (4) *persevere with hope* when she grows discouraged. Here are some of the amazing changes Linda began making in her life:

1. RELATIONSHIPS

Linda began to seek out and build relationships with other

women who were seeking God's best for their lives. Her faith began to grow as she surrounded herself with people pursuing the same goals as she.

2. GOAL SETTING

Linda began using simple goal-setting tools. She then graduated to more advanced methods that kept her accountable for the progress she wanted to make. It is human nature to slip to the lowest common denominator in the absence of accountability. And Linda refused to do that once she'd tasted change.

3. GRATITUDE

Linda began using the beginning and end of each day as a time to reflect on her blessings, to pray, to study her Bible, to write thank-you notes to friends. She found it much easier to remain positive when she stayed conscious of all she had to be thankful for.

4. GIVING

Linda and Victor began giving 10 percent of their income to their church and other causes that were making a real difference in peoples' lives. The principle of "You reap what you sow" is proven over and over in the lives of those who give of their time, talent, and treasure to others less fortunate. Besides, it's difficult to complain about your own situation when you constantly expose yourself to those who have even greater needs than you.

Linda Burzynski developed her faith, took action, is still learning, and has persevered with hope and the desire to please God. As a result, her plan to have a "better than good" life is succeeding.

If you will learn the disciplines of passionate planning, you will begin moving quickly toward peak performance. If you plan to be successful and trust God's leading as your plan unfolds, you, too, will live the "better than good" life.

7 | Setting Goals

I am only one; but I am still one. I cannot do everything, but still I can do something. I will not refuse to do the something I can do.
HELEN KELLER

If you chase two rabbits, both will escape.
PROVERB

Setting a goal is not the main thing. It is deciding how you will go about achieving it and staying with that plan.
TOM LANDRY

Aim at heaven and you will get earth thrown in. Aim at earth and you will get neither.
C. S. LEWIS

lorence Chadwick was no stranger to goal setting. An American swimmer, she was the first woman in history to swim the twenty miles across the English Channel from France to England (in 1950) and then a year later swim the same distance from England to France. And in 1954 she attempted unsuccessfully to be the first person to swim across Lake Ontario.

Between the English Channel successes and the Lake Ontario failure, Florence set yet another unbelievable goal: be the first woman to swim the twenty-one miles from Catalina Island to the west coast of California. On the morning of July 4, 1952, the ocean between Catalina and California was shrouded in fog—Florence could hardly see the boats accompanying her to keep away the sharks. Fatigue wasn't a big problem, but the bone-chilling temperature of the water was. After fifteen hours of nonstop swimming, she succumbed to the temperature of the water and asked to be pulled into one of the boats. Her mother and trainer, in a boat alongside her, urged her to keep on as they were getting near the coast. Yet all Florence could see was fog—she could have been twenty yards or twenty miles from the shore.

She was pulled out of the water too cold and tired to continue. Later, she realized that she was only half a mile from completing the swim and achieving her goal. When she learned how close she was when she quit, she blurted out, "I'm not excusing myself, but if I could have seen the shore, I might have made it!" It wasn't the distance or the cold that ultimately did her in—it was the fog. *When Florence Chadwick lost sight of her goal, she lost the will to continue.*

Here's the postscript: two months later, on a day when there was no fog in sight, she completed the swim, setting a new speed record for the Catalina-California crossing. Same island, same coast, same distance, same body of water. The only difference between victory and defeat was the ability to see her goal.

I share this story because it's like a prism—it reflects a number of different truths about setting goals. I'd like to share four of them with you:

1. FIND THE GOAL

There is no end to the kind and number of goals we can set in our lives. Florence Chadwick looked for things that hadn't been done in her area of expertise—first woman to swim the English Channel in both directions, first woman to swim Lake Ontario, first woman to swim from Catalina to California. Setting those goals forced her to continue to develop herself as a swimmer.

2. OVERCOME OBSTACLES TO THE GOAL

There are also any number of things that can derail our pursuit of a goal. We have to be informed and prepared in order to not be surprised when obstacles arise. It probably never crossed Florence Chadwick's mind that fog would keep her from reaching her goal.

3. KEEP YOUR EYE ON THE GOAL

Continual review and progress checks are critical. When we lose sight of the goal or it gets obscured by something unexpected, something happens emotionally. Keeping the goal in sight, literally and emotionally, serves to keep us energized.

4. SET AN ATTAINABLE GOAL

Fourth, goals can be ultimately achieved even if we fail the first time. There is a difference in swimming the Catalina-California crossing and swimming it on the first attempt. Failure to define the goal carefully can result in such discouragement, if we fail, that we won't try again. Fortunately, Florence Chadwick's goal was to swim the crossing, not swim the crossing on the first attempt—which allowed her to try again and succeed.

The Power of a Painting

Goal setters are picture painters. They are artists of life who use a canvas, brush, and paints to create images of what they want life to be like. But they don't paint literal pictures—they paint mental, spiritual, and emotional ones. They create images of how their lives will be different if they do thus and so, and it is those images that inspire them to set a goal and achieve it.

Goal setters often take the image they've created in their mind and reduce it to writing. They describe, in their own words, how life will be once their goal is reached. This verbal picture becomes a tool in their hand to review, amend, and expand while they are working toward their goal.

The power of a literal picture made the difference in my reaching a goal that had eluded me for many years. I had weighed well over two hundred pounds—way too much for my five-foot-ten inch frame—for far too long. I went on many different diets and periodically lost large amounts of weight, only to gain it back. Later I discovered that the problem had been with the picture I was painting in my mind.

When my youngest daughter was about five years old, I actually encouraged her to call me "Fat Boy." That was forty-five years ago, and I didn't know then what I know now about the power of pictures. I thought by encouraging my little girl to refer to me as "fat" I would be motivated to lose the weight. But it didn't work. All it did was reinforce in my mind the picture of myself that I hated—the overweight Zig Ziglar. As long as I kept the picture of me as a fat person in front of me, that was going to be how I saw myself. I could diet all I wanted and it wouldn't change a thing.

Things did change when I came across a new picture to replace the oversized picture of myself that was lodged in the "perception" part of my mind. I was at a doctor's office and saw a magazine ad showing a male model wearing the Jockey brand of men's undershorts. Most people know that the close-fitting "jockey" style of men's shorts aren't usually worn by fat boys. Indeed, the model in the Jockey ad I saw was (as you might suspect) trim and toned. He and I had relatively similar body types—the only difference was I had nearly forty extra pounds on my frame—not a pretty picture.

So I tore the page out of the magazine and taped it on my bathroom mirror where I was sure to see it several times a day. I began visualizing what my body would look like if it was as trim and toned as the man in the ad. I became convinced that it was possible for me to look like that. Indeed, I would look like that if I just lost the extra weight I was carrying and started exercising. That picture became my goal.

Once I had that picture in mind I set some subgoals: eating sensibly and exercising regularly. And—voilà!—in the subsequent months I lost the thirty-seven pounds that had made me a "Fat Boy." That was in 1972 and 1973, and I have stayed within five pounds of that weight to this day. The exercising and weight training I did changed some body fat to muscle, and I have been healthier ever since. At age seventy-four, on my last treadmill test, I stayed on the treadmill longer than I was able to at age forty-five when I was overweight and out of shape.

None of that happened until the picture in my mind changed. Once my body assumed the shape I wanted it to be in, I no longer needed a picture of someone else to stay motivated. I can see the picture anytime I want by simply looking in the mirror! I stay motivated to stay healthy because I have become comfortable with—and motivated by—my own success in achieving and maintaining a healthy weight.

On another occasion, several years ago my son and I were playing golf at a local club. On one of the holes, I got set to tee off but was careless in setting my stance. I hit the ball solidly but it sailed over the fairway fence, out of bounds. I marked down the two-stroke penalty and teed up another ball. I took my stance and announced that no way was I going to hit another shot out of bounds.

What was the picture in my mind at that moment? Hitting the ball out of bounds or hitting it down the middle of the fairway? My shot revealed the answer as the ball followed almost the exact path as the first shot—out of bounds. I had been picturing what I didn't want to do instead of what I did want to do.

The lesson? The same as with my losing weight experience: don't picture the negative, the thing you *don't* want to do or be like. Instead, paint a picture in your mind of what you want to achieve —what your goal will look like in your life when you reach it.

Those episodes taught me something critical about setting and reaching goals: keep a picture of the goal in sight. Florence Chadwick quit her quest for the California coast a half mile too soon because she lost sight of her objective. And you may abandon your goal before you reach it if you don't paint a picture of it and keep it in sight.

No Mountain Too High

Nobody illustrates the principle of painting a picture of your goals better than my friend Hugh Morton. Hugh's journey toward his ultimate calling in life was long and circuitous, and the goals he accomplished in the process will inspire you the same way they have me.

Hugh's first step required him to admit that he'd made a good, but not a winning, effort with regard to many things in his life—including his career. When he attended a class reunion in his late thirties, he was struck by how many of his former classmates had become doctors, attorneys, business executives, and members of other professions. They had established career goals and had achieved them. At that moment, Hugh Morton decided he needed to do the same.

Hugh was in bank management at the time and happened to receive a direct mail advertising piece for one of my tape series, *See You at the Top*. He bought it primarily for the bank employees to listen to but eventually listened to it himself. He heard about the need to have the right mental attitude and specific goals and discovered the difference between a good effort and a winning effort. In those tapes he heard about men like Walt Disney and Paul "Bear" Bryant—men who had failed many times and hadn't begun to accomplish things until they were forty years old. That gave him hope that it wasn't too late for him to set and achieve some goals of his own.

Because he had borderline high blood pressure in his thirties, Hugh established a goal to begin exercising and improve his health. He set a goal of being able to hike into and out of the Grand Canyon—a goal he shared with his family and several friends for purposes of accountability. After accomplishing that goal, he set a goal of hiking up Pike's Peak, which he accomplished in 1984.

In 1986 he found himself between jobs and with a family to support. He was at a low point in his life when he read that a small group was going to Nepal to the base of Mount Everest. So with his wife's blessings he made the journey—a trip that would change his life forever. Standing at the base of the twenty-nine-thousand-foot peak he knew he would never be content with his life until he someday made the effort to climb Mount Everest.

He began envisioning himself standing on top of Mount Everest. Seeing himself there was not a problem, but getting there was going to be a challenge. Hugh lived in Georgia where there are few tall mountains on which to learn to climb and even fewer mountain climbers or climbing schools from whom he could learn. So he started with what he had—small rock hills. This was a lesson in the need to take baby steps in order to reach an ultimate goal.

Perhaps you've seen the *Peanuts* cartoon strip in which Charlie

Brown is up to bat in a baseball game. He whiffs at the ball for the third time and slumps back to the bench. "Rats!" he says. "I'll never be a big-league player. I just don't have it! All my life I've dreamed of playing in the big leagues, but I know I'll never make it." The ever-ready-to-help Lucy turns to Charlie Brown and says, "Charlie Brown, you're thinking too far ahead. What you need to do is set yourself more immediate goals."

"Immediate goals?" Charlie Brown asks, looking at Lucy. "Yes," she replies. "Start with this next inning when you go out to pitch. See if you can walk out to the mound without falling down!"

That was exactly Hugh Morton's mind-set when he decided he wanted to climb Mount Everest: start with some pitcher's-mound-sized mountains and work his way up; achieve some immediate and intermediate goals before trying to tackle the ultimate.

Mildred McAfee said it as beautifully as anybody I've ever heard: "If you have a great ambition, take as big a step as possible in the direction of fulfilling it. The step may only be a tiny one, but trust that it may be the largest one possible for now." Do what you can now with what you have and what you know, and the more you use of what you know, the more effective you will be and the more your confidence will grow.

Hugh realized that each small goal he reached would give him encouragement, so he kept going. Eventually he met a local mountaineer, Mike Stewart. Hugh said, "He befriended me, and today he's still my climbing partner. Mike confesses now that he did not really think I was going to be able to do the things I wanted to do. He says he never told me that because he didn't want to hurt my feelings way back then."

Let me make a very strong point: *in the achieving of your goals, it's not what others believe you can do; it's what you believe you can do.* You plus God equals more than enough to accomplish your goals.

Hugh told me that a story he heard on my tapes greatly influenced him. This story was about a racehorse that, over the span of his career, won one million dollars in less than an hour of actual racing. On that tape I observed that you could take one hundred ten-thousand-dollar horses and buy them for one million dollars. But I said the one-million-dollar horse is worth more than a hundred ten-thousand-dollar horses because a one-million-dollar horse can run a hundred times faster than a ten-thousand-dollar horse.

Then I said of course that was not true. How much faster can the one-million-dollar horse run? Take one race as an example: The Arlington Futurity is one and one-eighth miles long, which, as everyone knows, is 71,280 inches. In this particular race, the first-place horse won one hundred thousand dollars more than the second-place horse. And the difference in winning and losing was one inch. In the 1974 Kentucky Derby, the winning jockey earned twenty-seven thousand dollars. Two seconds later the fourth-place jockey earned thirty dollars. Sometimes it's the tiny bit of extra effort that separates the winners from the second-place finishers.

Tiny differences can make huge differences in life. When a guy calls a girl a kitten, she'll love him; if he calls her a cat, he'll have a serious problem. Tell her she's a vision and she'll smile all over, but call her a sight and you won't get invited back. You can take tiny steps and score small points—but they add up. Hugh Morton's confidence grew with every small step, and that added up to big successes.

With every hill he climbed and every training goal he met, Hugh's ability steadily increased until, at age forty-four, five and a half years after he first stood at the base of Mount Everest, he could climb for seven or eight hours up a steep slope with a seventy-five-pound sack of concrete mix in his backpack. (During these years of rigorous training, by the way, his original high blood pressure disappeared and his resting heart rate dropped to forty-five to forty-six beats per minute.)

Hugh Morton laid a foundation for achieving his goal and eventually reached it. He conquered Mount Everest and went on, in time, to become one of just sixty-nine people from around the world to scale the highest mountain peak on each of the world's seven continents. That's what I call peak performance!

When Hugh returned from conquering Mount Everest, he decided to go into real-estate development and new home building. Since he had been a banker, he knew about money and mortgages but knew very little about building—not to mention the limited financial assets he had to invest. But he set a five-year goal to become the best home-builder on the south side of Atlanta. And in 1997, when the Metro South Chapter of the Greater Atlanta Home Builders' Association selected their first Builder of the Year, they chose Hugh's company. And he and his group went on to win numerous other industry awards.

Not surprisingly, he set more goals. In his own words, "We have continued to expand and have branched into mortgages, commercial real estate, and recently into bank ownership." His goals and his direction in business changed, but his objective to be the best and do the most with whatever he had never changed.

At age fifty-five, Hugh decided to pursue his long-time dream of learning how to pilot an airplane. Not only did he achieve that goal, but just two years after getting his private license he qualified for instrument flying, the hardest benchmark for a pilot to achieve. Success does breed success. It increases our confidence and keeps the fire burning.

Reflecting on his goal-based record of achievements, Hugh observed that building a lot of wealth was never his goal, but it happened as a by-product of pursuing with passion the goals that did mean something to him. Now a millionaire many times over, Hugh's material success has brought with it a desire to use his wealth for God's glory. To that end, among other charitable causes, he partnered with Rising Star Outreach and Women of

India to provide funding for a mobile medical clinic to treat lepers in and around Chenai, India. It is staffed by full-time medical professionals and has made a tremendous impact upon the health and welfare of this group of outcasts in India. This project, Hugh said, has brought him more satisfaction than anything he has ever done.

The Ultimate Purpose of Goals

Hugh Morton has proved that goal setting works. He was motivated to make changes in his life and accomplish some big dreams, personally and professionally. But there is something else that Hugh Morton's story reveals: the true purpose of setting and achieving goals.

The question "So what?" can be asked about any of our goals, and we ought to be able to answer it. Hugh initially began setting fitness and health goals that led, as I said, to his entrance into one of the most exclusive clubs in America: the people who have climbed the highest peaks on seven continents. In the process of accomplishing those goals, he learned a lot about himself and how to set targets and hit them.

When he returned to the business world, he began with an entirely different perspective: to attack his new business ventures the same way he did the business of fitness and mountain climbing—with passion. Because he did so, life rewarded him generously for his efforts. In fact, one of the awards his home-building company won was the coveted Summit Award (note the irony) given by the Professional Warranty Corporation for "Outstanding Customer Service and Satisfaction." In other words, Hugh Morton included in his quest for excellence a passion for taking care of the people his company served.

But the easiest way to answer the "So what?" question in Hugh Morton's life is the mobile medical team he funded to care for lepers in India. That is the ultimate purpose for achieving goals in this life: to serve and help others and make this world a better place to live.

I'm always impressed when I hear of a professional athlete or an entrepreneur who has established a foundation to use part of his or her hard-earned wealth to impact the lives of those in need. Whether it's a huge foundation that has given away billions to provide medical and educational services around the world or a smaller, community-based foundation that provides after-school activities for youth in a particular inner-city neighborhood . . . when people reach goals and life rewards them, a new and noble goal arises: share the wealth for the benefit of others.

Hugh Morton will tell you there was joy in getting his blood pressure down . . . joy in climbing Mount Everest . . . joy in reaching the summits of six more of the world's highest mountains . . . joy in building a profitable company providing houses that people could turn into homes . . . joy in learning to fly. But he will also tell you there has been no joy as great as giving from what God has blessed him with so that he might bless and serve others. That's the true and ultimate purpose of setting and reaching goals.

Could Hugh Morton have imagined that joy when he first set out to climb a rock hill in Georgia and become healthier? No way. But as he gave from his heart, a deeper understanding of the purpose of all he had accomplished became clear.

Here is the lesson to take from this chapter, my friend: you cannot out-give God! If you and I will use the resources He has given us—time, talent, and treasure—in ways that fulfill His purpose for our lives, He will keep opening doors and shining greater light on our path. He wants us to succeed! He wants us to meet goals that honor Him! And He wants us to honor Him by being conduits of His blessings. When we share with others what He has shared with us, we set in motion a chain of events that will allow others to begin setting and reaching goals themselves.

I can honestly say that those who pursue God's will for their lives don't always get everything they want, *but they want most of what they get.* In other words, because they were intentional about making sure that their dreams and goals conformed to what they knew of God's will at the time, whatever happened to them at the end of their journey is valued as God-given. Their attempt to do everything to the glory of God gives them confidence because they know that "God causes all things to work together for good to those who love God, to those who are called according to His purpose" (Romans 8:28).

When your number one goal in life is to die to yourself and put God first, you can rest assured you have set a goal that will last a lifetime—and then some. Pursue that goal, and every other goal imaginable will fall into place. You may never climb Mount Everest, but you will be a "peak" performer.

8 | Failure: Life's Refining Process

The men who try to do something and fail are infinitely better than those who try nothing and succeed.
LLOYD JONES

I don't know the key to success, but the key to failure is trying to please everybody.
BILL COSBY

Because a fellow has failed once or twice, or a dozen times, you don't want to set him down as a failure till he's dead or loses his courage—and that's the same thing.
GEORGE HORACE LORIMER

The girl who can't dance says the band can't play.
YIDDISH PROVERB

B ruce Larson's thesis is not the kind of thing that can be quantitatively verified, but I've seen enough real-life examples (including my own life) to believe he's right. In his book *My Creator, My Friend,* he makes this insightful statement: "Quite often the absence of immediate success is the mark of a genuine call."

Think about that for a minute. How many times have you witnessed a person who was a slow starter (translation: "failure") who later bloomed and became a raging success in his or her chosen field? More times than you can count, if you're like me. And I've read about countless others.

Take New England Patriots quarterback Tom Brady, for instance. By the age of twenty-eight, he had led the Patriots to three Super Bowl titles and been the Most Valuable Player in two of them. He's been featured on *60 Minutes,* hosted *Saturday Night Live,* had an audience with the pope, has a sixty-million-dollar football contract, and was invited to the 2004 State of the Union Address. But such was not always the case for this modest QB. Though he was an All-American high school quarterback, he received no attention at all from college scouts. If his father hadn't put together a videotape of Tom and sent it off to sixty college coaches, he might never have played college football. He was ultimately signed to play at Michigan but not as the starter.

When it came time for the NFL draft, the scouting report on him read, "Poor build, very skinny and narrow, lacks mobility and the ability to avoid the rush, lacks a really strong arm." He sat through six rounds of the draft before he was picked as the 199th player chosen—and again, not as a starter. When the starter for the Patriots was knocked out with an injury, Brady finally got his chance—and the rest is history.

Here's how Tom Brady sums up his slow start to NFL stardom: "Don't let other people tell you what you're capable of. As long as you believe in yourself and work hard to achieve whatever you set your mind to, you just keep plugging away. It may not be up to your timetable, but you can get it done."

Score one for Bruce Larson's thesis. In case you're not convinced, see if this name rings a bell (thanks to Mark Galli's *131 Christians Everyone Should Know*):

Johann Sebastian Bach settled in Leipzig, Germany, in 1723 after serving in a host of different musical jobs and positions. It's safe to say that he was not widely appreciated in his role as choirmaster of Saint Thomas's church and school. He and the town council were constantly at odds, and his musical genius was not appreciated by the rank and file. They thought he was stuffy and old-fashioned, stuck in obsolete and outdated forms of music. He was paid next to nothing (and when he died, authorities tried to defraud his widow of her meager inheritance).

But Bach labored on. During one period he wrote a cantata each week, 202 of which still survive. (A composer today would be considered productive if he wrote a cantata each year.) He also composed in Leipzig his famous Mass in B Minor, The Passion of St. John, and The Passion of St. Matthew—one of the most acclaimed works in the history of Western music.

After Bach's death, citizens in Leipzig seemed glad to be rid of him. When he was remembered, it was as an organist or harpsichordist, not a composer. Some of his music was sold off and some was even used to wrap garbage in! For eighty years, the music of Johann Sebastian Bach was neglected by the public. It was not until the German composer Felix Mendelssohn created an arrangement of The Passion of St. Matthew in 1829 that the compositions of Bach began to be appreciated. No one today would disagree that this eighteenth-century composer of more than one thousand works is among the greatest musicians in history.

When there are only a couple dozen NFL quarterback positions available, anybody who wants one but doesn't have one could be called a failure. And when there are only a handful of "great composer" labels available in Europe in the eighteenth century, any musician who doesn't have one might likewise be called a failure.

In light of these examples, let me give you a new definition of a "failure": a slow starter who refuses to give up; a slow starter who keeps doing what he is good at whether anyone recognizes it or not. That's why I like Bruce Larson's insight that the lack of immediate success is quite often the mark of a genuine call. That perspective keeps us from writing off people in our immediate-gratification culture who don't make a perfect score in life right out of the gate.

In fact, I believe there is a significant connection between passion, peak performance, and failure. Often, people with great passion for their calling will fail miserably at it before they achieve peak performance. Why? Because they often start too strong and fast. Maybe they lack the maturity that years of living will bring. Maybe they lack technical training or know-how. Maybe they lack experience. But they have so much passion that they rush out and trip all over themselves because they just don't know any better. Yes, they fail—but their passion keeps them in the game; they refuse to take no for an answer.

A classic example of this kind of person is the apostle Peter in the New Testament. Once he caught the big picture of what Jesus was all about, he came down with case after case of foot-in-mouth disease—speaking and acting on the basis of passion instead of propriety, falling and failing all over himself. But would anyone argue that Peter failed to become a peak performer? I doubt it! A quick perusal of the book of Acts in the New Testament shows Peter as a bold, wise, and courageous leader. For Peter, the formula of his life looked something like this:

Passion > Failure > Potential > Passion > Failure >
Maturity > Peak Performance

More and more through the years I have learned to watch for those people in whom I see potential but who don't seem to be performing up to speed or are even failing. I especially watch for those whose passion leads to massive failure. It's far easier to add experience and maturity to a person than passion. People who fail big are likely to succeed big, given time and opportunity. (Parents, take note!)

The Value of Failing

Failure is one of life's greatest teachers as long as we are not crushed by it—as long as we learn from it. I like to divide the world into two camps: learners and nonlearners. When the learners do something that is not wise, and failure is the result, they don't do it again. They learn the lesson. And when they do something that works, they take note and try to repeat it. In other words, they don't treat life like a tunnel—a tube that never gets narrower. They treat life like they're heading into a funnel. As they exclude choices and actions that don't work, they are continually narrowing the range of options: they're throwing out the stupid and keeping the stupendous. Eventually they hit their stride as peak performers because they don't do stuff that doesn't work.

The real question in life is not whether you are a success or a failure but whether you are a learner or a nonlearner.

Here are some of the best lessons to learn from failure:

- Failure teaches us to depend on God.
- Failure teaches us humility.
- Failure teaches us that we can't always get what we want.
- Failure teaches us to make a correction in our course of action.
- Failure teaches us character.
- Failure teaches us perseverance.
- Failure teaches us that we can survive.

Failure is a willing teacher, a master tutor. Anyone willing to sit at the feet of failure and soak up everything there is to learn will graduate quickly to the school of peak performance.

Eric Hoffer, who wrote widely on the subject of self-esteem, said, "In times of change the learners inherit the earth while the learned find themselves beautifully equipped to deal with a world that no longer exists." And speaker Steve Brown has said that anything worth doing is worth doing poorly—until you can learn to do it well.

Since most people fear failure like the plague, Steve Brown's words are good ones: they actually give you permission to fail. If you accept the notion that failure is just a pit stop on the way to the winner's circle, then you are prepared for the "better than good" life.

You Have to Start Somewhere

Our granddaughter Alexandra's dance recital began with little pixie-like three-year-olds who were having a ball. They were "failing" right and left, of course, because at that age it's a major accomplishment just to get them dressed and onto the stage in a semistraight line. Their primary strategy was to look at one another and do what the person next to them was doing. They didn't even know they were messing up, because they were trying so hard to please their teacher. At that age, there is no such thing as embarrassment, intimidation, or fear of failure.

Those little ballet prodigies were living, breathing examples of Steve Brown's words. It was worth letting them perform "poorly" because that put them on the path to learning to dance well. Very few times in life do we start out at the top of our game. We're like those three-year-olds in terms of our skill—unsure, unstable, unpredictable. Unfortunately, we're not like them in our self-analysis. We get so bound up with the prospect of failing that we won't even put our tutus on, much less take to the stage!

We have to start somewhere in life. If we would only grasp the idea that there are a certain number of compulsory hoops we have to jump through in life in order to be good at anything, we wouldn't fear failure. The quickest way to get one hundred steps down the road of life is to take step number one.

Once when legendary investor Warren Buffett was describing his investment strategy, he talked about the kind of old-fashioned financial analysis that every investor has to learn to do. Study the balance sheets and P&L statements and compute all the relevant ratios: price-to-earnings, price-to-book value, market capitalization, and the rest.

"But there are thousands of companies out there," someone asked. "How do you know where to start?"

"Well," Buffett replied, "you start with the As."

The sooner you get started pursuing your passion, the sooner you will fail. The sooner you fail, the sooner you'll learn what to do and what not to do. And the sooner you learn what to do, the sooner you can start doing it again and again.

Two Huge Failures

It would be hard to find two men who were as different as George Washington and Abraham Lincoln. Washington was an aristocrat—aloof and formal, difficult to get close to. Lincoln, on the other hand, was homespun and folksy, raised in poverty and possessed a dry sense of humor. Despite their differences, they are considered America's two greatest presidents. Both were God-fearing and devoted to their country and were models of integrity and honesty.

Another commonality between the two was their string of failures before achieving success.

You have likely seen a list of the ups and downs of Abraham Lincoln's career. In summary: he went to work for a businessman who went broke; he lost a bid for the state legislature; he failed in a second business attempt (and spent years paying off his and his deceased partner's debt); he ran for state legislature and won; his sweetheart died, which resulted in an extended depression; he was defeated in a bid to become speaker of the state legislature; he ran for Congress and lost; he was elected to Congress but lost his reelection bid; he was passed over for the job of land officer; he lost a senate race; he got less than one hundred votes at his party's national convention when he sought to gain the vice presidential nomination; he lost another senate race; and finally, he was elected president of the United States.

Abraham Lincoln failed to achieve most of the things he attempted to do in his life—but the most important one he achieved. Many scholars agree that Providence placed Lincoln in the White House to guide the country through the terrible years of the Civil War and the abolition of slavery. What might have been the outcome of those turbulent years had Abraham Lincoln concluded he was a failure after so many false starts and not run for president?

As for George Washington, he won only two battles as commander of the fledgling American armies in the Revolutionary War. One of the battles he won was the last one—the one that ultimately counts. The British drove Washington down through Long Island, into Brooklyn, across the East River, and up to Manhattan Island. They drove him on and on, but ultimately Washington was victorious. A few days later at Yorktown, General Cornwallis, the British general, surrendered to Washington. As he handed over his sword he said, "Sir, I salute you. Not only are you a great leader of men, but an indomitable Christian gentleman who wouldn't give up."

Washington and Lincoln teach us that Failure plus Perseverance equals Success! And if they were alive today and able to join us in conversation, I believe they would identify failure for what it is: an event, not a person or a way of life. But, you're thinking, when failures are strung together over years they can make it look like one's life is a failure. Right? Wrong! Failures happen one at a time, and each one has the potential to be the last. Failures have to be isolated and examined and learned from. They are not indicative of the value of the person or the effort that went into the attempt. They are what they are: something that did not work at that moment in time.

Let me give you two other examples of this truth:

Navy vice admiral James Stockton was a senior officer when he was captured and made a POW during the Vietnam War. He did not consider his captivity to be a failure on his part. He viewed it as an opportunity to continue doing what he had done through-out his career—providing leadership wherever he was assigned. That's exactly what he did in the infamous "Hanoi Hilton" prison in North Vietnam. After he was released, Stockton wrote that young people need to be taught that life is not fair and that fail-ure and adversity are things that happen, not ways of defining one's character.

He was right! A young person who fails a math test or acts fool-ishly is not a failure. He is simply a child who failed a math test or did a foolish thing. Stockton survived seven and one-half years, four of them in solitary confinement, by rehearsing in his mind the lessons he had learned about people who had faced adversity and succeeded: "The biblical story of Job reminded me that life isn't always fair. Even honest and upright men can be tested by evil and must be prepared to deal with it."

My granddaughter, Amey Fair, and her husband, Nathan, are full-time missionaries who serve in America and abroad. It has almost become a joke to them how many things happen to them just before they are to leave for an extended tour. Both of their cars break down, their children get sick, the dishwasher breaks, the computer goes on the fritz, plans they make unravel, they get irritated with each other, they run out of money . . . and on and on and on. They have learned to laugh at these events, which is what they are: events that don't go according to plan. It doesn't mean they are ineffective or failures as missionaries.

In their case, they believe there is spiritual warfare going on to try to keep them from succeeding in doing God's work. But they quickly learned to plan for these setbacks and overcome them. In their case, and in ours, faith, passion, and a willingness to learn and adjust will carry us through every time.

Stay the Course

If we added up the failures in our lives, we could easily be over-whelmed. Like Lincoln and Washington, men who failed at most of their endeavors, it only counts that we are successful at the really important times and places in life. The rest are learning experiences that prepare us for the crossroads events in life where succeeding really matters.

Babe Ruth struck out 1,330 times, but he also hit 714 home runs. Roger Staubach threw thousands of incomplete passes in his NFL career, but what most of us remember are the passes he completed that took the Dallas Cowboys to victory. R. H. Macy failed seven times before his department store in New York City finally caught on.

William Feather said, "Nobody succeeds in a big way except by risking failure." But legendary hockey star Wayne Gretzky—"The Great One"—said it best: "I miss 100 percent of the shots that I never take." The book we never write will never make it to the best-seller list. The worthwhile product will never catch on if the prototype is not brought to completion. The relationship will never develop or be mended if the effort is not made.

I'm personally convinced that not only is failure not a person, it is also not a crime. The crime is not making the effort—or having made the effort not seeing that effort through to completion.

I want to close this chapter by telling you about one person who failed to learn this lesson and one who did.

In 1846, Elias Howe received the first American patent for the lockstitch on the recently invented sewing machine. He was convinced this machine, coupled with his own enhancements, would rapidly improve the standard of living in countries around the world. Clothing and textile products would become less expensive and jobs would multiply. Unfortunately, America did not seem to agree with him. For whatever reason, he could not generate interest in the sewing machine.

So Elias Howe packed up his machine and headed to Europe, confident that this land of fine fabrics and sartorial splendor would turn into a gold mine for him. Alas, it was not to be. The Europeans were no more excited about the sewing machine than the Americans.

So what did he do? By this time he was so discouraged and out of money that he traded away all rights to the sewing machine to an umbrella manufacturer in exchange for a ticket back to America.

Had Elias Howe been in Europe a century later and had occasion to talk with Winston Churchill, he would have learned from the venerable prime minister that "success is often nothing more than moving from one failure to the next with undiminished enthusiasm." Elias Howe, at some point, stopped moving. His last failure became one too many, and he threw in the towel. He made the effort—but he failed to see the effort through to completion.

History abounds with stories of people who had something of real value but who gave up too soon. Yes, there are real obstacles: lack of money, lack of interest by others, lack of know-how. But those are obstacles that can be overcome, even if the project has to be set aside while one does something else to stay alive. As long as the passion is alive, there is hope. When the passion dies, the project usually fails.

Elias Howe released his dream too soon, but Ben Feldman was

an avid student who understood that dreams grow if you do. In the infancy of the life insurance industry, the only policies available were whole-life policies. And in East Liverpool, Ohio, there were not many people buying the five-thousand-dollar policy he was trying to sell. He loved the business and truly believed he had a product that could make a difference in peoples' lives. He was determined to stay in the business and make it a success.

One day it occurred to him that a larger policy might be more attractive to people seeking to protect their families and their interests. So he arranged to begin selling fifty-thousand-dollar policies and discovered they were no harder—and often easier—to sell than the smaller policies. And more profitable in terms of premium income. Over time, as he heard from families for whom the larger policies had been a godsend, his vision expanded—he added another zero and began selling five-hundred-thousand-dollar policies! To make a long story short, Ben Feldman eventually sold insurance policies as large as twenty-five million dollars.

Lest you think Ben Feldman was a graduate of all the Zig Ziglar sales-training seminars and was a super salesman, let me set the record straight. When he was invited to speak to the Life Underwriters Association, he would require that a large screen be placed between the podium and his audience. He was so shy he would not speak face-to-face to a large group of people!

Okay, so he wasn't a powerful public speaker. But he was honest, sincere, hardworking, creative, open to change, and willing to learn from what didn't work. And most of all he was passionate about life insurance. He was convinced people needed his product, and he stayed the course until he figured out a way to present it to them in the form that made sense to them. Before his career ended, Ben Feldman had sold $1.2 billion worth of whole-life insurance! And that was in a day when a billion dollars was worth something!

Someone has said that "Failure is the path of least persistence."

When you have a dream you believe in with all your heart, stay the course! Sometimes you have to take side trips and do other things purely to survive. Sometimes one more effort, one more month, or, in some cases, one more call might be the one that opens the door to success.

You have it in you to achieve peak performance in the arena of your dream. But only if you do not let temporary failures quench your passion.

9 | "Better Than Good" Habits

The strength of a man's virtue should not be measured by his special exertions, but by his habitual acts.

BLAISE PASCAL

Habit is a shirt made of iron.

CZECH PROVERB

What it lies in our power to do, it lies in our power not to do.

ARISTOTLE

Freedom is not the right to do what I want but the power to do what I ought.

BILL GOTHARD

I believe long habits of virtue have a sensible effect on the countenance.

BENJAMIN FRANKLIN

The best way to stop a bad habit is never to begin it.

J. C. PENNEY

I f you have spent any time in and around New York City, you
have probably seen and perhaps crossed the Hudson River on
the George Washington Bridge. The GWB is a suspension
bridge, meaning there are two large towers on either side of the
Hudson River, over the top of which are hung four huge cables
that are anchored in concrete and bedrock in Ft. Lee, New Jersey,
and the Washington Heights section of Manhattan. From those
four cables are suspended other cables that actually hold up the
roadbed of the bridge.

Without getting too technical here, I want you to absorb a few
numbers about those four massive cables. Each cable weighs
28,450 tons and is actually a bundle of smaller cables. To be exact,
each of the four main cables is a bundle of 26,474 wires that are
0.196 inches in diameter. (Think of a piece of thick rope that is
spun together from individual threads.)

So, the 4,760-foot-long bridge is held in midair by a total of
105,896 wires, each just under 0.200 of an inch in diameter.

The engineering behind that statement is more than my mind
can comprehend, but here is the question I want to pose to you: if
it were possible to begin to peel away those tiny wires, one at a time,
from each of the four main cables, how many wires would have to
be removed before the George Washington Bridge crashed into
the Hudson River?

Or, more to the point of this chapter, if it were possible to
begin building the bridge one tiny wire at a time, how many would
have to be added to each of the four cables before the roadbed
would remain solidly in place?

Theoretically—here comes the Ziglar Hypothesis of Habits—
the point would be reached where the addition of just one more
0.200-inch diameter wire would make the bridge immovable.
Think of the proverbial straw that broke the camel's back—theoretically, there is a "tipping point" where something becomes too
much. One more straw breaks the camel's back; one more wire

allows a bridge to be suspended in midair.

And I believe—theoretically, for the purpose of illustration—that at some point we cross a line in our lives where behaviors move from "act" to "habit." Granted, habits are much more subjective than the weights and measures of a bridge and its cables. But just as enough individual wires grouped together can hold a bridge over the water, so enough individual acts can create a habit that becomes unbreakable.

Habits are one of the critical components in the life of every person alive today. The problem is that habits can be good or bad, constructive or destructive, positive or negative, encouraging or discouraging. If you are going to live a "better than good" life, you must build as many positive habits into your life as possible. Think of your life as one of those giant cables on the George Washington Bridge and every individual wire as a habit. The more positive habits you bundle together, the stronger your life becomes—the more traffic it can bear, the more storms it can withstand, and the more service it can provide to others.

I have never known a true peak performer who did not invest consistent energy into the cultivation of good habits. Notice I didn't say "invest energy into getting rid of bad habits." Why? Because with the cultivation of every good habit (for example, getting plenty of rest at night) a bad habit disappears (sitting up watching late-night talk shows on television). It was the sixteenth-century scholar Erasmus who said, "A nail is driven out by another nail; habit is overcome by habit."

In this chapter we'll look at several habits I believe are indispensable in the "better than good" life.

The Habit of Staying Motivated

Motivation gets you going, but habit gets you there. When you make motivation a habit, you will get wherever it is you want to go more quickly and have considerably more fun on the trip.

Motivation has such a strong influence on our lives because it always precedes a decision, which is generally emotional. When decisions are consistently preceded by logical and inspirational input, a commitment that produces action is the result. In order for the action to be effective, the right kind of training or instruction must be applied. When the action is repeated regularly over a period of time, it will lead to a behavioral change. Behavioral change leads to habit formation, and winning habit formation means your chances of a "better than good" life are dramatically improved.

I am often asked at seminars, "Can everybody be motivated?" The answer is "Yes!" When we find people who are hard to motivate, it means we have not found, or they are not in touch with, their "hot button"—that emotional switch that is wired to their deep-seated dreams, desires, or calling. If we can find that hot button and then show them ways to accomplish what is important to them, they will be motivated. Once people learn the emotional and practical benefits of staying motivated, they will begin to motivate themselves—usually by developing some of the habits I'll talk about in this chapter.

The Habit of Listening

During the Lee Iacocca years at the Chrysler car company, my company did some training seminars for them. While I was there, I learned something valuable about the importance of listening.

Lots of innovations were taking place at Chrysler during that period, and many people were surprised at their source. Chrysler management went to the men and women on the assembly lines—the people who actually build the cars—and asked them for suggestions on how to produce a better car. And they got an earful about how the assembly lines were organized.

Back injuries (lost work time) were common among the assembly-line workers because they had to bend over to work on the cars as they came down the line. Other workers, who worked in pits beneath the assembly lines, complained of the dangers of slipping on constantly wet floors, resulting in falls (more lost work time). So management listened—and acted. In some places the assembly lines were raised to waist level so the cars could be worked on without having to bend over. And in other places the lines went over the workers' heads so they could work on the bottom of the cars, eliminating the dangerous pits.

As a result, absenteeism due to injury was cut dramatically and the expense of hospitalization and medical costs were cut by 90 percent. When employees were no longer falling and working with sore backs, morale increased. When morale increased, motivation surged and the quality of the cars coming off the line increased significantly. Quality went up, profits soared, and stockholders were ecstatic. As a result of listening to their employees, Chrysler started producing "better than good" cars.

Who would have thought there would be a connection between healing sore backs and ecstatic stockholders? And it happened because Chrysler took time to listen.

The Habit of Learning

Fred Smith says he has a right to not have a degree but he does not have a right not to have an education. George Eliot said, "It's never too late to become the person you could have been." And I have never seen that truth personified more clearly than in the life of Laurie Magers.

Laurie only finished the tenth grade. Twenty-eight years ago she came to work at our company as my secretary. In time, she became my administrative assistant, and today she is my I-don't-know-what-I'd-do-without-her executive assistant. A few years ago, while doing an evaluation of all our company's key personnel—and that definitely includes Laurie—she was rated at a level of effectiveness that suggested she had earned a master's degree.

Over the years, Laurie has taken classes and attended courses that continue to qualify her for more and more responsibility. She has self-educated herself to be increasingly more qualified to handle tasks that might have required years of formal education. Frankly, I'm amazed at what she can do.

For instance, no proposal leaves our company until Laurie Magers signs off on it. She approves every aspect of the print portion—language, style, grammar, clarity, and readability. Then she confers with accounting and checks any legal loose ends. Anything in written form involving company policy crosses Laurie's desk before it leaves our building.

Now how did someone with a tenth-grade education become qualified to do all that? Through the habit of learning. Laurie Magers has made learning a "habitual" part of her lifestyle. She reads, studies, questions, attends, critiques, inquires—she educates herself beyond her present responsibilities in order to become overqualified and ripe for a promotion. And she has been rewarded for her efforts.

Ask Laurie. She'll tell you it is not where you start—it's where you want to go and your willingness to work to get there that will make a difference. It's an established fact that earthquakes and hurricanes get all the publicity but termites do more damage than both combined. You, too, can experience radical growth in minute steps, just like Laurie did.

The Habit of Reading

In 2004 the U.S. National Endowment for the Arts published a study, "Reading at Risk," which reported that the number of Americans who read one book a year had dropped by 10 percent over the last two decades. The age group to show the largest decline in reading was the eighteen-to-twenty-four-year-old group, of whom 42.5 percent claim to have read one novel a year. These are disheartening figures.

For the past thirty years I have read an average of three hours daily, seeking information that will inspire, instruct, and encourage me so I can then use that same information to inspire, instruct, and encourage others. If an average reader (average is about 220 words per minute) will read twenty minutes every day, he or she will read twenty two-hundred-page books each year. Can you imagine the edge that would give them when it comes to effectiveness in our knowledge-based society?

For instance, Marie Wachlin of Concordia University conducted research among leading high school English teachers. What she found was that 98 percent of them believe biblical literacy gives students distinct educational advantages. Just reading the Bible—being biblically literate—was an advantage. That means you know what "the patience of Job," "the wisdom of Solomon," and "streets of gold" refer to. It means you are well-read, that you are familiar with the number one best-selling book in history—the book that is the basis for Western civilization.

Parents can do few things more important for their children than to raise them in a home filled with great books—and read those books to them! The love of reading is caught far more than it is taught. If you want your children to grow up to be readers, then they need to see you reading, going to the library, getting new books in the mail from book clubs or online retailers, and frequenting library book sales and garage sales looking for great, interesting books.

Consider this truism: the person who doesn't read is no better off than the person who can't read. We consider ourselves a literate nation, but is a literate nation of nonreaders really literate? Information is exploding so fast that anyone who does not read and keep up is rapidly falling behind.

Remember: readers are leaders and leaders are readers. And both experience a "better than good" life.

The Habit of Redeeming the Time

The average person in America today spends well over an hour a day in his or her automobile commuting to and from work. In some major metropolitan areas the drive time can be over two hours. Add to that the additional hours we spend in the car each week running errands, transporting kids to activities, going to church and other meetings—it's no wonder that the gap is narrowing between what we can do at home and what we can do in our cars.

With CD players, cassette players, and DVD players in our cars, now there is no end to ways to redeem the drive-time hours. You can listen to inspirational music, work through a collection of audiobook classics, even watch a motivational or instructional DVD if you're stuck in traffic. You can learn a new language—or teach your children a new language while you drive them to school each day.

I call this enrolling in Automobile University. And besides the intellectual stimulation and advances in learning you'll experience, there's another benefit: research shows you are four times less likely to be involved in an auto accident that causes you bodily injury if you listen to informative or inspirational material than if you talk on a cell phone.

Get smart, stay safe, and motivate yourself to become a peak performer.

The Habit of Doing Your Best

Why do companies all across America hire our company to come in and motivate their employees? Because so many people are not in the habit of giving their very best. In an economy that's growing (like America's is as I write) it's easy to get complacent, to do just enough to get by. That's a dangerous strategy for this reason: every day you go to work you are writing the work history that is going to follow you throughout your career. If you do poor work, that's what your boss is going to say when someone calls for a reference where you're applying for a new job. If you do mediocre work, that's what will be reported.

But if you do outstanding work—if you do your very best—your boss is going to be crying over the phone about how he hated to lose you . . . how he hasn't been able to replace you . . . how he tried to get you to stay . . . how he'd do anything to get you back.

Now, which kind of report would you prefer your former employer give about your performance? It is always in your best long-term interest to do your very best—to get in the habit of being a peak performer. And here's how:

1. THE "DAY BEFORE VACATION" PLAN

Let's say you're planning on going on a week's vacation beginning next Monday, so Friday will be your last day at work. Typically, late Thursday afternoon or evening, you'll make a to-do list of everything that needs to get done on Friday before you leave for a week. It's the only way to come back from vacation and not have your fellow employees mad at you because you left so many loose ends and irons in the fire that they didn't know how to deal with. Friday turns out to be a peak performance kind of day because you're so looking forward to vacationing in peace.

Question: why don't we operate that way every day? The "Day Before Vacation Plan" should be our daily approach to accepting responsibility and earning our pay—leaving work with everything taken care of that it was in your power to do.

2. THE "NO OTHER OPTION" PLAN

Perform on your job as if it were the only job available—as if the economy was terrible and you had no other place to work. If you work as if your job and your life depend on keeping that job (and doesn't it?), you'll strive to do your best daily.

3. THE "LIVE AND BREATHE THE JOB" PLAN

Do the little things that are not in your job description. Translation: take ownership! I played golf recently at a prestigious club where one of our foursome was the primary owner of the club. We all noticed throughout the game that anytime he saw even a small piece of trash he would pick it up. One of the other men made the comment, "You can always tell who the owner is."

When your employer sees you assuming ownership and responsibility for the company's image, reputation, products, and profitability, your value to the company will skyrocket.

4. THE "DON'T WORRY, BE HAPPY" PLAN

Get up on the right side of the bed every morning. Begin and end the day in a positive frame of mind. Greet your coworkers cheerfully in the morning and bid them good night in the evening. This is a habit that is easily cultivated. (Remember the "better than good" stories I told you in chapter four? It's infectious!)

5. THE "I AM WHO I AM" PLAN

Finally, live one life, not two. What you do in your private life, away from work, is just as important as what you do at work. In time, if you are living two lives, it will become evident. If I followed you around from the moment you left work until you returned the next morning—and did that for three months—I ought to see the same person in both places. Be true to yourself and those with whom you work.

The Habit of Health

Dr. Kenneth Cooper, the physician in Dallas who began the aerobics and fitness revolution, wrote a book called *It's Better to Believe.* He provides compelling evidence for the connection between the physical, mental, and spiritual parts of our lives. Concurring with Dr. Cooper is Dr. Herbert Benson of Harvard Medical School, who has identified what he calls the "faith factor" in physical and emotional healing: a strong personal belief system that accepts the importance of caring for the body and the practice of prayer and meditation as part of those beliefs.

The July-August 1995 issue of *Psychology Today* reported that a ten-year study of 2,700 people showed that, after accounting for risk factors, only one social attribute—church attendance—lowered mortality rates. Another study of elderly women found that the less religious had mortality levels twice that of the faithful.

Dr. Benson reports that patients with firm religious or philosophical convictions who practice the disciplines of meditative prayer tend to have more success in healing certain health conditions, including reducing high blood pressure, relieving headaches and backaches, and overcoming mental depression.

Consider making these six levels of purity—physical and spiritual—a habitual part of your life:

- Pure food: eat natural, wholesome, fresh foods.
- Pure air: don't use tobacco products; get regular aerobic exercise to increase oxygen flow.
- Pure water: decrease the amount of soda, caffeine, and alcohol you consume while increasing the amount of pure water and healthy fruit and vegetable juices.
- Pure soul: spend time with God, praying and meditating, reading His Word.
- Pure environment: create wholesome, uplifting, and healthy places to live.
- Pure body: detoxify; exercise regularly.

Health is holistic. You must seek to be healthy in all areas of your life if you are going to be a peak performer.

The Habit of Rest

Sleep, according to Forest Tennant, MD, one of America's foremost experts on drug addiction, is the only time the brain reproduces certain chemicals that are critical for keeping the body and mind balanced and in good health. If those chemicals are not produced and released during sleep, there are eventual symptoms that we try to alleviate with drugs (legal or illegal).

A lack of sleep results in poor decision making. There is evidence that the *Challenger*, Chernobyl, and Three Mile Island disasters were all caused in part by decisions made by people in critical positions who were suffering from sleep deprivation. I have seen my own work performance suffer as a result of insufficient sleep, which is why getting a good night's rest is a high priority for me.

Get in the habit of turning off the television and reading or listening to something positive and uplifting before falling asleep. And don't exercise vigorously within three hours of bedtime unless you want to be staring at the ceiling. The same goes for alcohol consumption.

Inadequate sleep impacts other areas of our life. If we're tired we're more likely to be irritable, to put off exercise, and to overeat. But if we've developed a plan for getting plenty of rest, we'll rise in the morning excited and ready to face a new day with a "better than good" perspective. Give your worries to God before you sign off at night and let Him work on them while you're sleeping deeply.

The Habit of Self-Discipline

When we were young our parents disciplined us. That doesn't mean they punished us (though they probably did that too). It means they trained us to be reliable and responsible. But when we are adults we have to discipline (train) ourselves to be peak performers. We have to hold ourselves accountable, set goals, and even reward ourselves occasionally for jobs well done. That is the essence of self-discipline: training ourselves in the habits of success.

It has long been known that people want off of welfare, they want to work, but they don't know how. They don't know how to be punctual, overcome obstacles, be dependable, follow through, and show up the next day. They are lacking the basic life skills that every child and young person is supposed to learn from his or her parents. They lack an understanding of the nobility of work—that flipping hamburgers at a fast-food restaurant can be noble work if the worker makes it so.

You may or may not see your daily work as noble. But you should (as long as it is moral and legal!). You can turn the lowliest job into the most honorable vocation through your own self-discipline—the development of habits and practices that make you the best there has ever been at that job. Peak performance has nothing to do with the job and everything to do with the person who is performing it—and how they're performing.

The Habit of Going the Extra Mile

I will tell you one brief story that will explain the habit of going the extra mile. On June 12, 2000, I checked into a Minneapolis hotel around 9:00 p.m. and began preparing for the following day's speaking engagement. I discovered that, for the second time in my career, I had failed to pack a necktie.

In a mild panic I rushed downstairs to the gift shop, which was closed. The desk clerks at the hotel told me there were no shops in the neighborhood open at that hour. I was stumped—until a young man working at the desk, with his supervisor's approval, offered to help. Jon Snyder lived a short distance from the hotel and offered to drive home and bring back several ties that would match my suit, from which I could pick one to wear the next morning. He returned promptly with a nice selection of ties, one of which worked perfectly, and the crisis was averted. Jon Snyder saved my life that night. I returned the tie to him the next day and sent him a nice gift when I returned home.

Need I say more? The Jon Snyders of this world are those people who are looking to serve others. As a result, they find themselves being rewarded with opportunity and advancement. Develop the habit of going the extra mile and you will be rewarded the same way.

The Habit of Pure Thoughts

There is such a thing as positive and negative imagination, moral and immoral imagination. Positive imagination is seeing yourself doing something good, noble, and successful. Negative imagination is plotting to pay someone back for something they did to you. Moral imagination is a young entrepreneur planning ways to set new standards for honesty and integrity in his industry. Immoral imagination is . . . Do I really need to give you examples of the immoral imaginations people have?

When it comes to imagination versus willpower, the latter almost always wins. If you're trying to break a bad habit (smoking, drinking, impure thoughts, overeating) and you put yourself in an environment that feeds your imagination, you'll likely succumb to the emotional pull of your thoughts. Alcohol, lottery, and casino commercials always picture the supposed upside of those endeavors, never the downside. Yet it is the downside that is reality. If you feed your imagination with those false images, your willpower will leak away like air out of a pricked balloon.

Dr. John Maxwell says, "You can spend your life any way you want, but you can spend it only once." And Carl Bard said, "Though no one can go back and make a brand-new start, anyone can start from now and make a brand-new ending." Remember: no one sets out to become addicted to nicotine, drugs, alcohol, sex, or gambling. It happens because of the power of negative or immoral imaginations. The only way to overcome that power is to fill your mind with positive and moral thoughts. Done consistently, those thoughts will eventually become your habit. As someone close to me who was trying to quit smoking said, "Don't entertain the thought." Eleven years after she quit, she is still not entertaining the thought.

I'm absolutely convinced that if we develop the habit of controlling our imagination and confine it to the good, pure, clean, powerful, and positive, we will embody what my mentor Fred Smith says everyone wants: not only will we live well, but we'll finish well.

Habits to Avoid

Instead of giving you a list of practices to avoid (you can probably guess what most of them are), let me give you some questions to ask yourself with reference to any negative practice that might become a habit in your life:

- Dr. Forest Tennant says that one out of every twelve people who take a casual drink will become an alcoholic. Are you sure you aren't that one?
- Dr. Tennant says tobacco is the gateway drug for many people into a lifestyle of addictive and destructive drug use. Are you sure it won't be for you?
- Would I want my behavior today to be the headlines in tomorrow's newspaper?
- Would I want my parents to know about my involvement with this practice?
- Do I plan on telling my spouse about my casual practice? If not, why not?
- Am I fooling myself into believing "This will never become a bad habit for me"?

As a young man I enjoyed not only the taste of alcohol but also the feeling that it gave me. I was driving home after a week on the road when I realized that I'd been in a bar every night the previous week. Truthfully, it frightened me, and I decided that night that alcohol was not for me.

Fortunately, alcohol never became a problem for me and I haven't had a drink since November 26, 1972, when the importance of the example I was setting became crystal clear to me. Drugs and alcohol extract a huge price in the lives of individuals and our nation as a whole.

My hope and prayer for you is that you will begin building into your life the positive habits that will, in time, replace the negative ones; that you will decide a life of peak performance is the life you are going to live; that you will leave behind those habits that will do nothing but keep you from reaching the heights God created you to experience. When you do, the "better than good" life will be yours, and richly deserved!

10 | The Power of Grit

What this power is I cannot say; all I know is that it exists and it becomes available only when a man is in that state of mind in which he knows exactly what he wants and is fully determined not to quit until he finds it.
ALEXANDER GRAHAM BELL

The secret of success is the consistency to pursue.
HARRY F. BANKS

With true grit you persist until you catch a glimpse of your potential. That is when passion is born.
FRED SMITH

Most of the important things in the world have been accomplished by people who have kept on trying when there seemed to be no hope at all.
DALE CARNEGIE

Press on. Nothing in the world can take the place of persistence.
RAY A. KROC

Never give in, never give in, never, never, never, never—in nothing, great or small, large or petty—never give in except to convictions of honor and good sense.
WINSTON CHURCHILL

My dream to be a speaker was born in 1952, when I heard Bob Bales speak in Florence, South Carolina. He gave me valuable direction, which I followed. However, it wasn't until 1970 that I was able to go full time in the business, and it wasn't until 1972 that my career as a speaker really took off. In those intervening years, I read a large number of excellent books and listened to outstanding speakers as I traveled countless miles driving to the "freebies" that I conducted. I also picked up examples, illustrations, and stories as I participated in a wide range of events.

I shared with audiences of all kinds and sizes. I spoke to civic clubs, Lions, Jaycees, Rotaries, schools, rehab centers, prisons, churches—to virtually any group who permitted me to share with them. I solicited feedback from those folks who were experienced in the field and who had my interests at heart. Through it all, I had some discouraging times when it seemed as though nothing was happening. But not only did I have the dream, the dream had me.

Along the way, I became convinced that what I had to say was important and that I could make a difference in people's lives. I can honestly tell you that not once did I ever contemplate abandoning the idea of being a full-time professional speaker. During those years, I continued to work in sales because, with a wife and four children, my first priority was to provide for them.

In retrospect, I realize that the long delay was largely responsible for much of the success I've enjoyed over the last thirty-three years. I was applying the principles on a real and everyday basis in my own sales life and in the lives of the people whose careers I was directing. I quickly found that the principles went far beyond the sales world. This revelation created a desire to discover more so that I could share more. Along this journey, I came to realize that the more I knew about my subject, the more creative I could be in my presentations. The more new ideas I acquired from others, the more useful my own ideas became, because truth forms a synergism. I was careful to seek truth and ethical principles as I built my career.

I believe that whatever your chosen profession, if you make a strong commitment and have a burning desire in your heart—combined with the conviction that you can make a difference—dogged persistence and grit provide you the best insurance for success. Remember that persistence enables you to develop other skills as you go along, provided that you're always "on the grow" and are genuinely passionate about benefiting the people you're dealing with.

Grit: The Story of Charles Goodyear

The next time you go to buy tires for your car, I hope the story I'm about to tell you will pop up on the radar screen in your mind and cause you to continue, finish, restart, or press on with your dreams. You may not buy tires made by the Goodyear company, but you'll likely see them as you shop—and when you do, I want you to think about Charles Goodyear. . . .

The best account of the life and quest of Charles Goodyear is called *Noble Obsession*, written by Charles Slack. I tell you that up front in order to make reference to the title. Normally, we think of an obsession in negative terms—the dictionaries define it that way: "compulsive preoccupation." And Charles Goodyear was totally, compulsively preoccupied with what he saw as his life quest.

But Charles Slack calls Goodyear's pursuit a "noble" obsession for a reason: Goodyear believed he had been called by God to solve a particular scientific problem. In other words, Charles Goodyear wasn't a nut (though he was accused of being one). He was simply a man who was passionate about what he believed was his purpose in life. For that reason, I believe there is much to learn from his story.

"Goodyear" is, of course, the Goodyear Tire and Rubber Company, founded and headquartered today in Akron, Ohio. But

Charles Goodyear didn't found the Goodyear company. In fact, he didn't even discover rubber as a natural product. European voyagers to the new world—Columbus, Cortés, and the like—found natives working with the gooey substance that oozed from jungle trees.

But Charles Goodyear was the link between a useless, sticky, raw material and the tires on your car, the sole of your running shoe, the eraser on your pencil, and the rubber bands that bundle your mail together.

When European businessmen learned rubber could be used as a waterproofing agent and could be shaped into other water-proof products like shoes and life preservers, they invested heavily—until the weather turned hot and the rubber became soft, gooey, and formless. The "rubber fever" of the 1830s ended as quickly as it had begun. Numerous rubber companies that had sprung up went out of business and investors lost millions. The conclusion was that rubber was worthless.

Charles Goodyear wasn't so sure. As a habitual tinkerer and former inventor, he was curious as to why rubber could not be fashioned to resist heat and hold its shape. So in 1834, Charles Goodyear began an odyssey that consumed the rest of his life. He spent every penny he had on thousands of failed experiments. He sold off the family furniture and dinnerware to raise money. He went to jail several times for failure to pay his debts. But he never gave up.

Then in the winter of 1839 he hit pay dirt. He had mixed raw rubber with white lead and sulfur and discovered that the sulfur caused the rubber to hold its shape, even when reheated. He had discovered the process now known as vulcanization—the basis of the modern rubber industry.

But fame and fortune still eluded him. He spent several more years trying to perfect the process while all the time mired in lawsuits against those who falsely claimed they had invented the rubber-sulfur combination. He and his family constantly faced financial ruin until he died in 1860. And even five years later, the patent he had eventually been granted expired, and his discovery entered the public domain.

In 1898, Frank and Charles Seiberling formed a rubber manufacturing company in Akron, Ohio, and named it Goodyear Tire and Rubber Company in honor of the discoverer. They used his discovery and began manufacturing tires for bicycles and the growing automobile industry.

Charles Goodyear's story is a powerful one—the man was true grit personified—because of his raw determination. But it's all the more compelling for readers of this book because of its connection to passion and purpose. Goodyear was an avid Bible student and faithful church member who believed his "noble obsession" was a calling from God. He would not be stopped in his pursuits, because he believed he would then be unfaithful to God's purpose for his life. It takes that kind of passion and purpose to reach the levels of peak performance I'm describing in this book.

Destiny and Determination

In *Noble Obsession*, Charles Slack made this observation: "About the only uncomplicated thing in Charles Goodyear's life was the clarity of his mission. He never wavered, never thought seriously of giving up. The worse things became, the stronger his resolve grew. He did not seek poverty, yet neither did he shy away from it. He explained in his memoirs that God had chosen him to solve the rubber mystery and that he, Goodyear, was merely 'the instrument in the hands of his Maker.'" His certainty about that, Slack continues, "gave him a rare and awesome strength."

Later in this book I will delve into the power of purpose—and specifically, a sense of divine purpose—in our lives and its ability to take us beyond what we think we're capable of. But with specific reference to determination and grit, nothing can make us more determined to perform at our peak than a sense of purpose. My heart breaks when I think about the number of people who get up and go to work every day without a sense of purpose. They see themselves as nothing more than a cog in a machine, easily replaced by another cog should they drop out. They aren't determined to do their very best, or to see their dreams fulfilled, because they see no ultimate purpose, bigger than themselves, in what they are doing. If, however, one believes in a personal destiny, then determination and grit replace apathy and a sense of insignificance.

It was a sense of purpose that drove Charles Goodyear to pursue his dream of making rubber a valuable product for the world. Perhaps many people have drawn this connection, but it is the words of Martin Luther King Jr. that I recall first: "If a man hasn't discovered something he will die for, he isn't fit to live."

Criticism and Determination

Once when Charles Goodyear's wealthy brother-in-law told him that rubber was dead and he needed to give up his quest, Goodyear replied, "I am the man to bring it back." Charles Goodyear was impervious to criticism; he refused to believe 1) that rubber had no practical value and 2) that he was not the man who would discover it.

Let's be clear about criticism and determination: it's possible that determination can turn into bull-headed stubbornness. The Bible, in the book of Proverbs, calls those who refuse to listen to counsel "fools" (Proverbs 12:15; 15:5). The challenge we all face is this: how do I know when my determination to succeed has moved beyond healthy stick-to-itiveness and moved into unhealthy, obstinate stubbornness? I can't answer that question for you or anyone else. There are far too many variables involved in each situation to reduce determination to a formula.

But this I do know: the world is full of naysayers and

pessimists. Our determination should never be squelched by those who have no other reason for criticizing us other than their own opinion of what is possible. To the degree their opinions are backed with healthy amounts of wisdom based on experience, facts, evidence, or sheer volume, they gain credibility. It is up to every person who is the target of criticism to consider the source and weigh the merits.

But it is not criticism based on evidence that I find most destructive; it is emotional criticism. Let's face it—none of us likes to be called stupid in so many words. Our egos are fragile (unfortunately) and can be the weakest link in our chain of determination. When our ego is bruised, our determination can lose its power in a heartbeat. Our internal self-esteem message system immediately communicates, "You are being rejected by others because of your dogged determination to see this project through. Give up the project and you'll once again be accepted."

Have you heard that voice before? Of course you have, and so have I. It's at that point that a little self-talk—or a conversation with a trusted mentor or friend—is required in order that the "Don't give up" voice can drown out the "Give up" voice. Three times in the book of Psalms we find the psalmist engaging in such self-talk: "Why are you in despair, O my soul? And why have you become disturbed within me?" (Psalm 42:5, 11; 43:5). He counseled himself about the realities of his situation and decided the facts didn't warrant despair.

In a December 2005 article in *Psychology Today*, author Peter Doskoch discusses one of the most critical environments on earth: "Beast Barracks" at West Point, the United States Military Academy. There are several goals for the summer preceding the first academic year at West Point, not the least of which is to weed out those who are not strong enough mentally to take four years of rigorous discipline. Therefore, everything is criticized: one's appearance, attitude, skills, physical abilities, mental acumen, and emotional toughness. As a result, as many as 5 percent of every year's entering class of plebes packs it in and goes home before the school year begins. Doskoch relayed this fact: "A grit questionnaire administered to all 1,223 cadets entering the class of 2008 showed that grit is the single best yardstick for predicting who will survive the academy's punishing first weeks."

The cadets who survive Beast Barracks no doubt do so because they are determined not to be broken by the criticism leveled at them by their upper-class handlers. You can survive your own version of Beast Barracks if you will resolve the same thing: "It's not personal—'life' is trying to break me, to see if I can make it. So I will prove that I can in spite of the criticism and attacks that come my way."

Creativity and Determination

As I have already mentioned, Charles Goodyear was not a scientist and had no laboratory experience. In other words, he had no innate "talent" by birth or training to predict that he might be successful in what he wanted to accomplish. If, as I believe, grit is the bedrock of success, this should not surprise us. And we should also not be surprised that recent research suggests that a mere 25 percent of the differences between individuals in job performance can be attributed to IQ. Intelligence accounts for only a fraction of the reason for success. Grit has value for people at all levels of ability.

This is true even for geniuses. Mozart's diaries, for example, contain the familiar passage where he says that an entire symphony appeared intact in his head. But no one ever quotes the next paragraph where he talks about how he took the next several months to refine the work.

However, while it is true that study after study of high achievers in various fields shows that the one common characteristic of their success was that they were tenacious, these same studies suggest that determination motivates people to incredible feats of creativity.

Goodyear's tenacity motivated him not only in trying to find a way to make rubber hold its shape when heated, but in other areas as well. He used various methods for raising money—borrowing, profit-sharing, partnerships, investors. There was nothing he was not willing to try to keep his dream alive. I've never met a peak performer yet who didn't possess an undying conviction concerning how to go around, through, over, or under an obstacle that stands in the path leading to success.

Barbara Corcoran sold her New York City real estate company in 2001 for $70 million. Not bad, considering she began it with a $1,000 loan twenty-five years earlier. But she came close to losing it all following the stock market crash of 1987. She owed $300,000 and was writing a good-bye speech to her employees when she remembered something from her childhood. Her grandfather's neighbor had had a litter of four puppies to sell and invited a crowd of interested buyers to come at one time to look at them. Supply and demand took over. Since there were only four puppies and three times that many interested buyers, every one became the pick of the litter.

Corcoran set her good-bye letter aside, added up the value of the eighty-eight different apartments her company had for sale in seven different buildings, divided the total by eighty-eight, and priced them all equally regardless of size or shape. She then ran an ad announcing the once-in-a-lifetime opportunity. Hundreds of people lined up to get one, and she netted over $1 million in one weekend. "I was able to open up two more offices in the depths of the recession. The worst hours became the best hours, simply because of persistence," she said.

In keeping with the Peter Doskoch article in *Psychology Today*, the persistence Barbara Corcoran displayed was essential to her success, but it would not have helped without her business-saving spark of creativity.

Most great achievements in life do not occur "inside the box." When Jeff Bezos founded Amazon.com, he attracted hordes of buyers with creative innovations—and his creativity has continued unabated: one-click buying, free shipping, gift wrapping of purchases, customer reviews of products, ability to purchase a used book or CD cheaper than a new one, and on and on.

Get outside the box on your quest—only there will you likely find the creative ideas you need for the breakthrough you are seeking.

Time and Determination

When Charles Goodyear set out to solve the rubber problem, he placed no time limit on his venture. Because, as I have already mentioned, he believed God had called him to his task, he viewed it as a lifelong commitment. It so happened that his discovery of what would ultimately be known as vulcanization happened in five years, but he literally spent the rest of his life trying to perfect and bring to market what he had discovered.

Are opened-ended dreams more noble than closed-ended ones—those with time limits? Absolutely not. You may set a goal to reach a certain weight within one year, or earn your PhD degree within five years, or save ten thousand dollars to start a new business within twenty-four months. A classic example of a closed-end goal was President John F. Kennedy's announcement to Congress, on May 25, 1961, that America would land an astronaut on the moon by the end of the decade. That goal was achieved on July 20, 1969, when *Apollo 11* commander Neil Armstrong set foot on the moon's surface.

But some dreams and goals do not work well with timetables. Take Princeton mathematician Andrew Wiles's quest to solve the 350-year-old math problem called Fermat's Last Theorem. He was ten years old when he first encountered the math problem and decided he would be the one to solve it. Throughout his youth he worked on the problem and continued, as his teaching responsibilities would allow, as a professor of mathematics. In 1986, he buckled down. Seven years and fifteen thousand hours of intense research later, the theorem was solved. "I wasn't going to give up. It was just a question of which method would work," the shy mathematician said.

Peter Doskoch cites what experts call the "decade rule"—meaning that "it takes at least a decade of hard work or practice to become highly successful in most endeavors, from managing a hardware store to writing sitcoms—and the ability to persist in the face of obstacles is almost always an essential ingredient in major achievements."

The interesting phenomenon regarding the decade rule is this: looking ahead, ten years looks like forever. Looking back, it seems like the blink of an eye. Therefore, don't let the "long haul" dissuade you from reaching your goal. When you get there, you'll remember little of the blood, sweat, and tears you expended. You'll be basking in the rarified air of success as you stand on the performance peak toward which you've been traveling.

Permission and Determination

Charles Goodyear didn't ask anybody's permission to solve the rubber-hardening problem. Who in the world is "in charge of rubber"? Granted, there may be times when permission is needed if your goal infringes on the life or rights of other people. But even if such is the case, here is my final admonition from the life of Charles Goodyear: don't take no for an answer. In the vast, vast majority of cases in life, only one person's finger is on the accomplishment switch regarding your goals: yours. As long as you don't flip that switch (say no to yourself) it will stay on and your quest will continue.

There is power in grit, my friend. The next time you shop for tires or put air in your own, remember Charles Goodyear. This unlikely inventor discovered something that changed the world at the turn of the twentieth century—because he refused to give up on his dream.

Passion without determination will only find the nuggets that are lying on the surface. If you expect to find anything more valuable, it will take passion plus determination. Nobody lives the "better than good" life without determined digging—the kind God made you capable of. So begin today and don't stop until you arrive at your destination!

11 | Redefining Success

Whatever the place allotted to us by Providence, that for us is the post of honor and duty. God estimates us not by the position we are in, but by the way in which we fill it.

TRYON EDWARDS

God does not want us to do extraordinary things. He wants us to do ordinary things extraordinarily well.

BISHOP GORE

If at first you do succeed—try to hide your astonishment.

HARRY F. BANKS

If at first you don't succeed, try hard work. . . . Success seems to be largely a matter of hanging on after others have let go. . . . There isn't much thrill in success unless one has first been close to failure.

WILLIAM FEATHER

In 1950, The Redhead, our daughter Suzan, and I lived in Florence, South Carolina, where I worked for the Wearever Aluminum Company. I was in direct sales, putting on cookware demonstrations in homes each evening for groups of couples.

My wife purchased tickets for us to hear a motivational speaker named Bob Bales—an event that proved to be life changing for me. He was doing what I do now—traveling all over the country encouraging and inspiring people to be and do their very best. I had never seen anybody have so much fun and at the same time do so much good and, I thought, make so much money—all of which appealed to me. So The Redhead and I persuaded Mr. Bales to go to dinner with us that evening. During that time I asked him what I needed to do to become a speaker as successful as he was.

I was only twenty-five years old at the time—a little young, Mr. Bales thought, for people to take me seriously. So his first piece of advice was for me to have some more birthdays. Second, he suggested I set some sales records to establish credibility as a persuader. Finally, it was he who encouraged me to go work for the Dale Carnegie Institute to gain more experience and credibility in my chosen field.

Everything he said made sense to me, so I set out to accomplish all three of his suggestions. There was nothing I could do to speed up the birthdays, so I focused first on my sales. I had already done well, but I redoubled my efforts as a salesman and sales manager with the goal of setting new records within the company. Which I did. When I eventually wrote to the Dale Carnegie people five years later, I described in glowing terms what I had achieved in sales—and they offered me a job. I accepted their offer and promptly moved our family to New York City.

What Is the Price of Success?

The transition from my childhood in Yazoo City, Mississippi, to my new workplace in New York City was culture shock. But I loved my work—promoting their sales program—and felt that I was making a significant contribution. (For years after I left, they continued using some of the strategies I implemented while I was there.)

But there was a downside to the success I was experiencing in New York City. I would leave home every morning while my wife and daughters were still sleeping and would not get home at night until after they had gone to bed! This was not something I had anticipated, and it violated a heartfelt priority in my life: spending quality time with my wife and children. I concluded that if being successful in New York City required that kind of sacrifice, it was a price I was unwilling to pay.

One of the ways I knew it was time to leave makes me smile all these years later when I think of it: Friday night was the only night of the week I was not conducting training classes. After we'd been in New York almost three months, I came home one Friday evening and found that we had been invited next door to a cook-out with the neighbors. When it came time to leave later that evening, my oldest daughter, who was five, turned to the neighbors and called out, "We'll see 'youse' guys later!" When I heard that, I turned to The Redhead and said, "Pack our bags, Mama. We're going home." My southern roots just couldn't handle my daughters losing their charming southern vernacular at such a tender age! So, after just three months, we moved back to South Carolina.

Still, our time in New York and my experience with the Dale Carnegie Institute were valuable in many ways. I feel that what I learned from the experts there definitely contributed to the success of my career. And the experience helped me solidify, at a young age, the order of my own priorities in life—and my family was at the top of the list. I've tried to be careful ever since not to strive for any level of success that had a price tag I was unwilling to pay. When I became a Christian on July 4, 1972, my first priority became my relationship with Christ, then my family, and finally my career. Since then every facet of my life has been dramatically better.

The price of success can be too high. I've learned that success takes patience and persistence—that it doesn't happen overnight. And I've learned that there are some levels of personal success I'm simply not interested in—those that cause me to be a failure in my relationship with God or my family. For me, true success is knowing God is pleased and my family is happy and secure. Nothing I could do without those two realities would be considered a success in my book.

Success and Limitations

John and Randy Davis have been in wheelchairs almost half their lives, put there by the effects of muscular dystrophy. John was diagnosed at age two, Randy at age five. Despite their disease they were determined to live full lives—specifically, to become Eagle Scouts.

To gain the rank of Eagle in the Boy Scouts program requires earning twenty-one merit badges in a wide range of fields. The Boy Scouts of America has a program for disabled Scouts that allows them to work on alternative kinds of merit badges suited to their abilities. But John and Randy chose not to apply for the alternative program. "We wanted to see how far we could get without it," Randy said. Paul Schieffer, Scout master of Troop 1103 in Dallas (a troop for disabled Scouts), said the brothers worked at first on the same merit badges. But as they got older and their interests began to vary, they chose different paths.

Seven years after attending his first meeting John became the first member of Troop 1103 to become an Eagle Scout. A year later, Randy became the second. "Maybe it will give other kids some inspiration," said John. "Even if you don't make it, it's worth the trip." Message: John and Randy had a disability, but they were determined that the disability would never have them.

I can imagine that during the seven or eight years it took the boys to succeed at their goal, they grew weary. The accomplishment makes me think of the Robert Strauss quote, "Success is a little like wrestling a gorilla. You don't quit when you're tired—you quit when the gorilla is tired."

The problem with reaching for our goals is that goals never get tired. They stay right there on the horizon forever, waiting for us to reach them. Therefore, the challenge is for us not to give up the pursuit of success. If we grow weary and give up, the goal remains for someone else to achieve. John and Randy are outstanding examples of what it takes for any person to be successful.

Besides, who among us is not disabled in some way, even if it's not physical? I don't know any perfect people, especially the one I see in the mirror every morning. I may not have a disability like the Davis brothers, but I've got plenty of others in the mental, spiritual, and emotional realms of life. And so do you! Therefore, what the Davis boys did—succeed in spite of severely limiting handicaps—is exactly what we all have to do: succeed in spite of whatever limitations (disabilities) we possess.

Somehow we think it's fantastic when people like John and Randy succeed—as if that's what disabled people are supposed to do: overcome their disabilities. We read about them in magazines or see their stories on television and marvel at their determination. We think that having a disability makes them stronger. Please don't read their story and think they are special except in the sense that the more severe one's disabilities, the more we admire one's success. Look at them as models for all disabled people . . . which is all of us. They only did what every successful person is supposed to do: persevere and pursue our dream until we reach it and not let limitations of any sort hold us back. That's what folks who want the "better than good" life do.

Success and Criticism

I have read that the average person thinks he or she is twice as likely as everyone else to obey the Ten Commandments. And it doesn't surprise me at all. There is an incredible self-serving bias built into all of our psyches. We all think we're wonderful! The truth is, however, that such biases are a great impediment to genuine maturity. We ought to take Socrates's advice to "know thyself" more seriously.

When we have too lofty a view of ourselves, it is difficult to engage in healthy self-criticism or to receive criticism from others. And, as Socrates (again) said, "The unexamined life is not worth living." While that may be an overstatement, I get his point—and agree with it. How will we be able to correct something in our life— a hindrance to our success—if we don't know it exists? Proverbs 29:23 in the Old Testament says, "A man's pride will bring him low, but a humble spirit will obtain honor." If we're too proud (if we think too highly of ourselves) to recognize our own faults, we're not likely to ever reach increasing levels of peak performance.

On the other hand, there are some people whose mission in life is criticism—not of themselves, but of others! They look for faults as if there is a reward for them. The *Beaumont* (Texas) *Enterprise* newspaper of May 17, 2005, carried a story of a classic example of how successful people learn to ignore destructive criticism.

Kim Mulkey-Robertson became the head women's basketball coach at Baylor University in 2000. The year prior to her arrival, the team had won just seven games. But in 2005, Kim led the Lady Bears to a 33-3 record, beating three divisional number-one seeded teams to win the national championship. Even after compiling that record in 2005 she received critical E-mails. One self-appointed critic chastised her for failing to recruit one partic- ular player a few years earlier: "If you had signed this kid a couple of years ago, you'd have gone undefeated."

There's no pleasing all the people all the time. Criticism is a reality of life. Successful people find the balance between ignoring and accepting criticism. I try to take my mother's advice in this area: consider the source. If the criticism comes from a source you respect, receive it and give it your consideration, and don't be afraid to agree with it and make the changes suggested. But if the criticism is negative and destructive and self-serving (to the other person), put it out of your mind and move on. Listen to the encouragers, not the unfair, unreasonable critics in this world. Those people who are interested in your living a "better than good" life can be your greatest friends—welcome what they have to say. Those who are jealous of your success or caught up in petty pursuits—forgive them and move on.

There is one Person whose evaluations I strive more than any to receive. I want to hear Him say, "Well done, good and faithful servant" (see Matthew 25:21 NIV). Because I know He loves me and wants what is best for me, I will listen to anything He has to say.

Character and Success

Allow me to repeat a question I first posed in my book *Over the Top*: how is it that a total population of three million people was able to produce George Washington, James Madison, Benjamin Franklin, John Adams, Thomas Jefferson, and a host of other luminaries with the moral and mental capacity to draw up plans for the greatest country in the history of civilization? I believe the credit goes not so much to these individuals but to the character of the population as a whole. In other words, the Founding Fathers were a reflection of the people from which they were drawn.

And what was the source of such character? There were two primary sources: the Bible and the *New England Primer* that was used in America's schools for over two hundred years. From the *New England Primer*, first graders were taught B-I-G words—words of four, five, and six syllables. Looking in the *Primer* I see words

like *gratification, edification, abominable, admiration,* and *beneficial*—
words that were associated with character, either good or bad.

Also in the *Primer,* lessons were tied to the Bible. For instance,
letters were learned by memorizing biblically-based rhymes:

A: In Adam's fall, we sinned all.
B: Heaven to find, the Bible mind.

The biblical basis for character was taught to all children who
learned to read and write. The Bible and the *New England Primer*
were the two indispensable tools for educating the youth of the
new country called America. In fact, the Continental Congress
purchased twenty thousand Bibles to distribute to citizens who did
not have their own.

According to the Thomas Jefferson Research Institute, in the
first two hundred years of our country's history over 90 percent of
the educational thrust was of a religious, moral, and ethical nature.
By 1950 the religious, moral, and ethical content in the curriculum of public schools was so small that it could not be measured.
By 1960 we had become anti-Christian, particularly in the media
and in many of our educational institutions. Tolerance has
become our nation's new religion. Today we tolerate everything
with the exception of Christians and Christianity.

Without the biblical benchmark, character has wandered
from pillar to post in America over the last fifty years. America's
corporate and government landscape is littered with the moral
and ethical failures of leaders in recent years. I don't believe it is
possible to be truly successful without possessing moral character
and values that are consistent with the time-honored traditions of
the Bible.

The Founding Fathers got it right when they built America on
the solid foundation of God's Word.

Tolerance and Success

One of the greatest disasters of our time is our universal acceptance of *tolerance* as a great virtue. It's lauded from the big screen and little screen as well as in the print press—we mustn't be judgmental; we must be tolerant of other people and their points of view.

The reality is that all of us are intolerant of many things. For example, should anybody be tolerant of the child abuser, the wife abuser, or the concepts of the Ku Klux Klan? Should we really be tolerant of anyone's right to say and do anything they believe is right? Should we be tolerant of the views of the Nazis or the Communists, or of those who believe we should all "do our own thing," regardless of the damage to other people? I recently received a letter from a gentleman who criticized me for my lack of tolerance—and yet his criticism of my lack of tolerance concerning a certain issue revealed his own intolerance.

Dr. William Bennett wrote a book called *The Death of Outrage* in which he asked why we are not speaking out loudly and forcefully about the deterioration of the values being taught in our society. Why are we not more outraged over child abuse, wife abuse, drunk driving, and a host of other societal ills? Why don't we rise up, express our outrage, and get angry about anything anymore? Why aren't we motivated to encourage others to take action on these things that are destroying our society? Dr. Martin Luther King Jr., the leader of the civil rights movement until his untimely death, said, "Our lives begin to end the day we become silent about things that matter."

I believe the problem is our confusion between "tolerance" and "an open mind." I have an open mind as far as the acceptance of people and ideas until it becomes obvious that their ideas are either illegal, immoral, or unethical. Example: I would not defend the rights of a pedophile, and I hope and believe that your tolerance level would also be zero. I would be tolerant of the pedophile's right to a fair trial, but intolerant of his right to continue to abuse children.

Message: keep an open mind, be tolerant of the rights of others to believe what they believe, but if what they believe violates the laws of God and/or man, I encourage you to be intolerant. When the laws of man run counter to the laws of God, we have stopped being tolerant and have become sinful. And we need to know the difference. Tolerating behavior that flows from sinful character establishes a precedent that leads to moral deterioration.

What does tolerance have to do with your long-term success? Tolerance is a reflection of character. When we tolerate the wrong things, it is an indication of a flaw in character. And no structure built on a flawed foundation will stand the test of time. If we want to reap the best out of life, we have to sow the best. The Law of the Harvest is this: we reap what we sow. If we sow actions based on moral and ethical character, we will reap a harvest based on the same. And character always lasts; it stands the test of time and will endure. Like the house Jesus taught about in the Gospels, the house built on solid rock endures the storms while the house built on sand does not (see Matthew 7:24–27).

In March 2005 my associate Krish Dhanam and I had a marvelous experience conducting seminars in India. I was concerned about many of my Western figures of speech not translating well to the Indian audiences—especially my biblical references, since most of the attendees were either Hindu, Buddhist, Jewish, atheist, or Muslim. Their verbal response—zero. But when newspaper reviews of the seminars appeared in local papers, they were very complimentary. It was only after returning home that I realized why: I had taught biblical principles and God's word does not return void regardless of your belief or lack of belief. The Bible is the foundation for Western civilization, English law, and most of the great moral and social reforms in Western history.

When E. D. Hirsch Jr., Joseph Kett, and James Trefil published *The Dictionary of Cultural Literacy—What Every American Needs to Know* in 1988, the first twenty-six pages of this reference book were given over to the Bible. Unfortunately, cultural literacy changes, and I'm not sure the Bible is holding its own in American culture as a need-to-know reference. If it loses its place, our culture will be the real loser, for we will lose the influence of God and the moral and ethical benchmark by which American society has been measured since the Pilgrims stepped ashore in 1620.

I encourage you to be one of the ones that ensures America's success in the future by keeping biblical morality and values at the heart of your quest for success.

Family, Friends, and Success

My own father died when I was just five years old. But my heavenly Father stepped in to assist my mother, who had a fifth-grade education and six of twelve children still too young to work. Because of the kindness of Mr. John R. Anderson, who ran a local grocery store, my younger brother and I went to work before we were really able to be of much help. He was a successful business-man of impeccable character, and he had such a huge positive impact on me that I gave my son his first name. By successful, I don't just mean materially. I mean he was the kind of man a young boy could model his life on.

Mr. Anderson and his meat-market manager, Mr. Walton Haining, were both godly men who showed me what it meant to be a person of character—to be honest and accountable and hardworking. God provided these men in my life at a time when my own role model, my father, was taken from me. I don't know how I would have turned out had these two men not impacted my life so deeply at a young age.

A primary responsibility of the older generation is to impact the one coming after by modeling integrity—to be there to teach and support and assist the rising generation to become all it can be. The whole world saw a touching illustration of this at the 1992 summer Olympics in Barcelona, Spain.

Derrick Redman was running the 400-meter sprint for Great Britain when he pulled a hamstring muscle in the home stretch. I've read that this is one of the most painful injuries a runner can experience. Indeed, Derrick Redman was knocked to the ground. He got up and began hobbling, essentially on one leg, toward the finish line. Derrick's father, Jim, was watching the race from along the home stretch. He climbed over a fence, ran to his son, and put his arm around him, and together they hobbled toward, and crossed, the finish line. The picture of this father helping his son to finish the race became an iconic image of that Olympics.

While that picture speaks to the way earthly fathers help their sons, it has a broader meaning to me. It speaks of how my heavenly Father came into my life when I was young and wounded by the loss of my own dad and provided two godly men to be models of character and success for me. While I didn't realize their impact at the time, looking back I am aware of how important they were in my life. Child psychologists tell us that the vast majority of a child's personality and character formation takes place in the first six years of life. How thankful I am to have had two good men to step in where my father left off and help keep my life on course.

I have wanted my life to count in a similar fashion. Through my speaking, writing, and lifestyle I have hoped to model the kind of character that would encourage others in a godly and successful direction. I am thankful for those who have told me that something I've said or taught, or just the way I live, has had a positive impact on their life. To me, that is part of a successful life—being a model for those who come after.

Don't fail to include "role model" as one of your marks of success, starting with your own children. None of us is perfect in this regard, but we need to strive to be and learn to ask forgiveness when we aren't. Every life that is "better than good" will instill a hunger for a "better than good" life in others.

Success Personified

Booker T. Washington was born a slave on a southern plantation but rose to become one of the most highly respected men of his day and one of the most highly regarded educators of all time. As founder, first teacher, and president of the Tuskegee Institute in Alabama, he did more than any person of his time to help his race overcome the devastating effects of slavery and regain hope for the future.

Dr. Washington's attitude about slavery was remarkable: he believed adversity increased one's ability to concentrate and reach desired goals. He said, "I have learned that success is to be measured not so much by the position that one has reached in life as by the obstacles which he has overcome while trying to succeed." He believed complaining about one's situation, about unfairness or the lack of opportunity, was a sure way to remain miserable and poor. His motive was to inspire black students to look beyond their circumstances and see that success was possible.

Here, in his own words (from the excellent *Up from Slavery: An Autobiography*), is Booker T. Washington's philosophy:

I am constantly trying to impress upon our students at Tuskegee and on our people throughout the country, as far as I can reach them with my voice, that any man, regardless of color, will be recognized and rewarded just in proportion as he learns to do something well, learns to do it better than someone else, however humble the thing may be. As I have said, I believe that my race will succeed in proportion as it learns to do a common thing in an uncommon manner; learns to do a thing so thoroughly that no one can improve upon what it has done; learns to make its services of indispensable value.

Dr. Washington stressed doing one's very best right where he or she is. That is what is necessary for survival at times, and it certainly was necessary for him at his time in American history, as well as necessary for those he taught. But once we have stabilized ourselves through hard work, a positive attitude, and a lack of complaints, we can begin to look at the next step on the ladder. Growth means more than survival—it means success. And with success comes significance.

Everyone, Dr. Washington believed, wants an opportunity to succeed, and life is governed by immutable laws of God that will grant success to everyone who applies him- or herself. No man, he believed, who continues to add something to the material, intellectual, and moral well-being of the place in which he lives is left long without proper reward. This is a great spiritual law—the law of reaping what we sow—that cannot be permanently nullified.

When we lose ourselves in a life work—something bigger than ourselves—Dr. Washington taught, we forget about the pursuit of happiness from a selfish point of view. In time we realize that we are truly happy and content because of the contribution we are making to something important. To the degree one loses himself in this way, in the same degree does he get the highest happiness out of his work.

The greatest pursuit in which the human being can lose himself is the glory of God. When we seek that which pleases Him, He promises to bless us. I can think of no higher definition of the "better than good" life, no greater definition of success, than to live a life blessed by God.

PART III:
THE PURPOSE OF THE
"BETTER THAN GOOD" LIFE

12 | What Is the Purpose of Life?

Get the pattern of your life from God, then go about your work and be your-self.
PHILLIPS BROOKS

Purpose is the place where your deep gladness meets the world's needs.
FREDERICK BUECHNER

He who has God and everything has no more than he who has God alone.
C. S. LEWIS

For a small reward, a man will hurry away on a long journey; while for eternal life, many will hardly take a single step.
THOMAS Á KEMPIS

The chief end of man is to glorify God and enjoy Him forever.
THE SHORTER CATECHISM (1646)

Great is the art of beginning, but greater is the art of ending.
HENRY WADSWORTH LONGFELLOW

In November 2005 you may have seen and heard the media coverage about the issue of "Intelligent Design" since it played a prominent role in a couple of state and local elections (Kansas was "for" it; a town in Pennsylvania was "against" it). Even if you missed the coverage of those elections, you are likely hearing lots of buzz about this subject.

I want to note something interesting about the Intelligent Design argument that relates to what I believe about purpose in life. First, to summarize, the Intelligent Design movement grew out of the efforts of part of the scientific community to find evidence in nature that "Someone" or "Something" designed our universe. In other words, the Intelligent Design proponents do not believe in evolution—the theory that life began accidentally and that the universe (and our planet) continues to evolve on a random, unguided basis.

One of the leading spokespersons for the Intelligent Design movement is a scientist named Michael Behe, a PhD biochemist at Lehigh University in Pennsylvania. In his book *Darwin's Black Box: The Biochemical Challenge to Evolution,* he asks us to consider a traditional mousetrap. It's a simple device—a wooden base, a wire hammer that delivers the blow, a strong spring, a catch that releases the spring-powered hammer, and a metal bar that holds the hammer back until it is released by movement of the catch. Got it? We've all used one of these simple devices to catch a mouse (and probably a finger or thumb in the process).

Every part of the mousetrap has a purpose. In fact, if you take away any one of the parts, the mousetrap will cease to work. Likewise, if you separate the mousetrap into its individual parts and scatter them around your garage, no mice will be caught. (The parts are useless on their own as far as mouse catching goes.) Because every part has a purpose, the parts have to function together in order for the mousetrap to work.

Now, here's the question the Intelligent Design movement

asks: how did the parts of the mousetrap come together to form a device that accomplishes its purpose? Evolutionists say they came together by accident or chance; Intelligent Design proponents say the existence of the parts working together presupposes the presence of a "Designer" who put them together.

Mousetraps are only an illustration—obviously, man is the designer of the mousetrap and all other mechanical devices in our world. But Behe uses the mousetrap illustration to suggest that the infinitely more complex chemical and biological "devices" in nature—things at the molecular level that Charles Darwin didn't have electron microscopes to see—could never have come together to accomplish their purpose in sustaining biological life without a Designer.

And here's the bottom line: the very existence of so many wonderfully working biological creations in our world just shouts out the word *purpose* to me! And I include you and me in that list of purposeful creations. My mind simply cannot comprehend how anything as unique and intentional as all the aspects of our creation could have just "happened" into existence. And if all our parts have purposes, that suggests a purpose for the whole, meaning your life and mine.

Behe's mousetrap illustration makes pretty good sense to my nonscientifically trained mind, and it seems to fit perfectly with something I read in the Bible about my life: that God created me, part by part, to accomplish a purpose in this life. Take note of the words of the psalmist:

For You formed my inward parts;
You wove me in my mother's womb.
I will give thanks to You, for I am fearfully and wonderfully
  made;
Wonderful are Your works,
And my soul knows it very well.

My frame was not hidden from You,
When I was made in secret,
And skillfully wrought in the depths of the earth;
Your eyes have seen my unformed substance;
And in Your book were all written
The days that were ordained for me,
When as yet there was not one of them.
(Psalm 139:13–16; emphasis added)

If it takes a human designer to create the parts for a mouse-trap all at the same time and fasten them together to accomplish a purpose, how much more reasonable is it to think that the psalmist's perspective is accurate about humans? A mousetrap has a half dozen parts—my body has trillions of living cells, millions of which will die and be replaced while you are reading this chapter. Within those trillions of cells there are innumerable chemical processes going on, every second of every hour of every day.

When I think about the "mouse catching" going on in my body at this very second, I am forced to agree with the psalmist's further thought:

How precious also are Your thoughts to me, O God! How vast is the sum of them! If I should count them, they would outnumber the sand. When I awake, I am still with You. (Psalm 139:17–18)

I am forced to conclude that there is a Grand Designer who created me, and you, who put all the parts together in a common fashion for all human beings, yet did it in a totally unique fashion so that no two of us are alike. I've been told the world couldn't handle another Zig Ziglar—and it's a good thing, since there's not another one! Nor is there another you!

And if every part of our body has a purpose (yes, even our

tonsils and appendix), then it stands to reason that God created us for a purpose. And it is that purpose every person needs to discover.

Passion, Peak Performance, and Purpose

I've been talking in this book about the "better than good" life. So far we've talked about the first two components of that life: passion and peak performance. And if you have bought into what I've said about those two Ps, then you're all dressed up, needing a place to go! And that's where purpose—the third P—fits in. Without purpose in life we are like the proverbial fool who is all dressed up with no place to go. We're firing on all cylinders, working at maximum proficiency, but we're spinning in circles.

Passion supplies energy and drive, and peak performance is the result of the application of passion. But without purpose, peak performance becomes a hit-or-miss affair. By that I mean that most people could probably find several things in life they could do pretty well. In fact, most people are performing at an acceptable, even high, level of performance in the jobs and vocations they are currently pursuing.

But it's my contention that peak performance in life only comes when I'm exercising my passion toward that which I believe is my purpose in life. And, by that definition, I think many people in life have never tasted peak performance. Why? Because they have not searched for and discovered their purpose. And that may be because they never knew, or chose to believe, that they *have* a purpose in life! And that's what I hope to change in your thinking in Part III of this book—to motivate you to believe that you have a purpose in life.

"But wait, Zig," you might say, "I get bonuses every year, have been steadily promoted in my job, and get great reviews. I even like my job for the most part. Why wouldn't you consider that an example of peak performance?"

Let me answer that question with a few questions of my own:

Would you sink into deep despair tomorrow if you were told you can no longer work at your present job? Would you keep doing what you're doing at half the salary? Are you going to continue what you're doing because you have to (financially) or because you want to (you can't see yourself doing anything else)? Regardless of how well you do your current "thing," is there something you dream about doing that's completely different—something you hope to do when you retire and can "do what I really want to do"?

How you answer those questions has a lot to do with whether you're performing at your peak, because they have a lot to do with whether you think you're accomplishing a divine purpose for your life or not.

Look at these diagrams to get a visual picture of what I'm saying about passion, peak performance, and purpose:

The Way a Lot of People Live

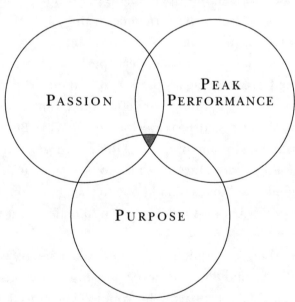

There is only a small area where passion and peak performance overlap with purpose.

The Way Every Person Should Live

PASSION, PEAK
PERFORMANCE,
AND PURPOSE ARE
ONE, NOT THREE
SEPARATE PARTS
OF LIFE

Obviously, I've used the extreme ends of the spectrum to illustrate my point: there is probably more overlap between passion, peak performance, and purpose in most people's lives than is pictured in the first diagram, and 100 percent unity of the three dynamics, as pictured in the second diagram, may not be achievable in this life. *But 100 percent overlapping of the three is still the goal we are striving for.*

Now, picture in your mind an infinite number of diagrams in between the two that show increasingly more overlap of the three areas as you move through life. Hopefully, that's what's happening to each of you as we come closer and closer to achieving peak performance in what is our true purpose.

In fact, on the following page, draw three circles that represent your life. Position the circles to overlap in a manner that represents how you see yourself in your life at present. (Use a pencil.) To what degree are passion, peak performance, and purpose moving toward becoming a unity instead of three separate dynamics?

Passion, Peak Performance, and Purpose: How I See My Life

_____

(Today's date)

You might want to come back to this diagram in a couple of years and erase the circles you drew and draw three new ones to see what progress (or regression) you've made.

Life is a journey toward wholeness . . . toward passion . . . toward peak performance . . . toward purpose. As you change and adjust your life through the years, and these three dynamics move ever closer together, the quality of your life will be increasingly "better than good."

The Power of One

When I speak to an audience of thousands of men and women at a time, I am always struck in a fresh way about this idea of purpose. The very fact that people would take a half day or full day off work and pay their hard-earned money to come and hear me and others speak about purpose, motivation, potential, success, and numerous similar subjects says one thing to me: people care!

Somewhere, in each of our heart of hearts, we know we are supposed to excel, to "do better," to reach our goals, to accomplish significant things, and to be peak performers. Nobody is forcing people to come to these seminars, just as no one forced you to buy this book. But you're just like me—you want to be all you can be. Otherwise, you wouldn't bother. You'd just dawdle along in third gear all your life without a desire in the world to shift into overdrive. I guess there are some people out there like that (after all, not everyone comes to hear me speak!). But I believe something happened to them along the way. Somehow the flame of purpose that burns in the heart of every person got doused with a lethal dose of negativity or criticism or abuse or discouragement. Somewhere along the way they gave up and threw in the towel and said, "Why bother?"

May I ask you a personal question? Is it possible that you are in that camp—that you're reading this book as sort of a "last gasp"? If we were sitting in a quiet coffee shop talking together, I would want you to tell me if that's how you felt. And I can promise that you wouldn't get a lecture in return. In fact, you'd get the opposite. You'd hear an "Amen, brother" or "Amen, sister" from me, because I know that feeling. I know it's possible to get so discouraged that you wonder if you'll ever succeed at being and doing what you want to be and do.

There was a time in my life when I wondered if I would ever get it together. And had I not come to know God in a personal way and reoriented my thinking around Scripture, I might not have. And if He hadn't given me The Redhead to pray for me and encourage me along every step of the way, I would not have accomplished what I have. So I know the feelings of discouragement that can come our way in this life.

But here's what I would tell you: if it weren't possible for you to be and do what you were created to be and do, you wouldn't feel bad about not doing it! You wouldn't care! The very fact that we're sitting together talking about your purpose in life is evidence that you know the difference between succeeding and not succeeding. The fact that you're at a place right now where you think you've failed is a positive sign! That means you know the difference between winning and losing. And as long as you know the difference, there is every possibility in the world that you can turn your failure into success, that you can find your purpose in life and achieve it. These aren't word games, friend—it's the truth! You are one person in this great big world, but you were created to occupy a unique place. Right now, your chair is empty because you're struggling with whether it's worth trying to fill. But no one else can or will. If you don't grab hold of the purpose God created you to achieve, it will be a tragedy! We, the rest of us, need you to accomplish your divine purpose.

Here's something else that I know happens at my seminars. (I know because people have told me.) Invariably, in a crowd of thousands there will be some individuals who will look around at all the Thoroughbreds gathered in the hall and say, "Man, I'm the old gray mare or the broken-down stallion in this bunch. What chance do I have of succeeding against this kind of horsepower? And who would miss me if I just enjoy Zig's talk and decide not to take it any further?"

There is awesome power in every single person created in the image of God. If you don't think so, look at the difference one person has made throughout history:

- In 1645, one vote gave Oliver Cromwell control of England.
- In 1776, one vote gave America the English language instead of German.
- In 1845, one vote brought the state of Texas into the Union.
- In 1868, one vote saved President Andrew Johnson from impeachment.
- In 1875, one vote changed France from a monarchy to a republic.
- In 1945, one vote saved the Selective Service System just

twelve weeks before Pearl Harbor was attacked.
- And, unfortunately, in 1923 one vote gave Adolph Hitler control of the Nazi Party in Germany.

Those are just a few instances in which one person has made a huge, inestimable difference for good or, in some cases, for bad in the affairs of this world. At the time the people casting those votes did so, they likely didn't realize the ramifications of what they were doing. Rarely do we have that kind of insight at the time we act. But from the perspective of history, our actions have unbelievable consequences. We cannot see into the future, but we can have faith that the acts God calls us to accomplish are significant and meaningful and need to be carried out. Remember the words of the psalmist:

> *Your eyes have seen my unformed substance; and in Your book were all written the days that were ordained for me, when as yet there was not one of them* (Psalm 139:16).

God sees everything at once and knows what you are called to do. Our part is not to *play* God but to *trust* God—to believe that our single, solitary life can make a difference.

Christopher Wren, who designed the magnificent St. Paul's Cathedral in London, was one of the greatest of all English architects. One day, after work on his cathedral had begun, Wren walked unrecognized among the artisans and stonecutters. "What are you doing?" he asked one of the workmen.

"I am cutting a piece of stone," the man replied.

He put the same question to another.

"I am earning five shillings two pence a day," the man said.

He asked a third man the same question, and the man answered, "I am helping Sir Christopher Wren build a magnificent cathedral to the glory of God."

The third man had a purpose! He could see beyond the cutting of stone, beyond the earning of his daily wage, even beyond a single work of art. With the eye of faith, with the benefit of perspective, with the confidence of his calling he saw a grand cathedral being built. His foresight is all the more commendable in light of the fact that St. Paul's took thirty-three years to build. It's possible that workman never saw the actual finished building—but what he saw through the perspective of purpose was all he needed to treat his task as a high calling, not just as a job.

You are not just "one"—you are a significant one with an important purpose to fulfill.

Purpose and Permission

If you're ever approached by a young man named Kyle Maynard who asks you if you want to wrestle, my advice is, don't!—even though he has no arms below the elbows or legs below the knees. Kyle Maynard is a congenital amputee—a condition that affects one in every two thousand births, but rarely in as extreme a case as Kyle's. He has only the upper part of both arms and the upper part of both legs, yet he became a championship wrestler in his Georgia high school. The title of his new book, *No Excuses* (September 2005), pretty much says it all. His parents raised him not to make excuses, and he's made none.

As a kid, Kyle was all about sports. He played goalie in street hockey games with his friends, and even played on a football team in the sixth grade. He also started wrestling in the sixth grade— and lost his first thirty-five matches. But by the time he got to high school, it was a different story. He and his father, a former wrestler, had worked out a weight-training program that made all the difference, and he and his coach worked out new moves and holds unique to his physical condition. In his senior year on the varsity wrestling team, he won thirty-five matches and lost sixteen. He qualified for the state championships and won his first three matches—but lost his final match (wrestling with a broken nose) in a thriller.

Kyle drives his own car, now attends the University of Georgia, and has more plans for the future than seemingly any five people could accomplish. His parents stressed living a "normal" life when he was growing up, which seems to be what he has done. When asked to define what "normal" means, here's what Kyle Maynard said: "To me it means just to go about things day to day as if they don't matter, as if the obstacles I face aren't there. Leading a normal life doesn't mean living a stagnant life. You're going to look ahead and you're going to set your impossible goals that other people would say you can't achieve. And you can go out and do it."

After describing Kyle Maynard to you, I hardly think anything more needs to be said about self-esteem. Unfortunately, however, there are lots of people with no physical challenges who don't view themselves as "normal" as this congenital amputee does. What does it take to see ourselves in a positive light—to have a positive self-esteem—in spite of the limitations and difficulties all of us experience? What does it take to believe that we are significant enough to have a purpose to fulfill?

The answer to that comes from a great story in the Old Testament. A spiritual leader named Samuel had been sent to the village of Bethlehem to identify and anoint the man who was to become the next king of Israel. He knew this man was one of the sons of Jesse, but he didn't know which one. Jesse had eight sons, seven of whom stood before Samuel when he arrived. But God said none of them was the new king. The youngest, David, was out tending sheep, so Samuel sent for him. When he arrived, God said, "Rise and anoint him; he is the one."

When Samuel was being told no concerning the first seven of Jesse's sons, here is what he heard from God: "Do not consider his appearance or his height, for I have rejected him. The Lord does not look at the things man looks at. Man looks at the outward appearance, but the Lord looks at the heart" (see 1 Samuel 16).

So what is the key to a healthy self-esteem? Looking at yourself the way God does, not the way this world does. If Kyle Maynard's parents and coaches had used the world's standards to determine Kyle's worth, and then communicated that worth to Kyle, where do you think he'd be today? Kyle's mother said, when Kyle was a baby, "All we knew was that he was a beautiful baby. He was glowing. He was gorgeous. . . . So we focused on his face, that gorgeous face."

Can you find the key word in her description: It's "glowing." Glow in any of our lives comes from the heart, not from our physical appearance. When Kyle's parents saw him, they saw life and potential! And that's what they communicated to him. And guess what? Kyle believed them and became one of the most emotionally healthy young men you'd ever hope to meet.

My friend, there may be many things in your outward life that the world would tell you are not "normal." You may lack education or money or status or experience or picture-perfect looks. (That was me sixty years ago—and I still don't have the picture-perfect looks!) But so what? God doesn't care about any of that. Remember: "Man looks at the outward appearance, but the LORD looks at the heart" (1 Samuel 16:7).

Did you ever see the little buttons that were popular a few years back that said, "God Don't Make No Junk"? That's the absolute truth and the key to the self-esteem of every person created in the image of God (which is all of us). If there is some part of who you are that you are ashamed of, embarrassed about, or wish you could change, think carefully. God looks at your heart and accepts you completely for who you are—and so should you.

All you need to find and accomplish God's purpose in your life is God's permission and approval—not anyone else's. When you get in step with Him, there will be a glow on your face that will make people wonder what you're up to. It will be the glow that comes from fulfilling God's purposes in your life when no one else thought you could.

As you read the rest of Part III on purpose, remember the lesson of the mousetrap: you have been put together by an Intelligent Designer in order to accomplish something grand. When you combine your purpose with your passion, peak performance will be the result. In other words, the "better than good" life!

13 | Discover Your Calling

If a man is called to be a street-sweeper, he should sweep streets even as Michelangelo painted, or Beethoven played music, or Shakespeare wrote poetry. He should sweep streets so well that all the hosts of heaven and earth will pause to say, here lived a great street-sweeper who did his job well.

MARTIN LUTHER KING JR.

The responsible person seeks to make his or her whole life a response to the question and call of God.

DIETRICH BONHOEFFER

Each honest calling, each walk of life, has its own elite, its own aristocracy based on excellence of performance.

JAMES BRYANT CONANT

Life is not just a few years to spend on self-indulgence and career advancement. It is a privilege, a responsibility, a stewardship to be lived according to a much higher calling, God's calling. This alone gives true meaning to life.

ELIZABETH DOLE

Readiness and ability for any work is not given before the work, but only through the work.

ANDREW MURRAY

We could count on one hand the number of people in history whose calling in life was handed to them on a silver platter—like a telegram arriving from heaven. A somewhat larger number have had a "Eureka!" moment in which they somehow knew what they were called to do for the rest of their lives. But for most of us, discerning our calling in life is a process, something that becomes clear over time.

There is no right or wrong way to figure out one's calling. Self-examination, counsel, prayer, experimentation—all of these are helpful. But there is one principle I have found to be true: the more you know about your purpose in life, the easier it is to separate callings into the "Yes" and "No" piles.

Here's an example: In *Discipleship Journal,* Kevin Miller writes about a time when he was invited to join the board of directors of a large ministry organization. He was thrilled with the opportunity. For him, it was a no-brainer—something he wanted to start yesterday. But as he talked over the opportunity with his wife, the practical side of the opportunity became clear. Saturday board meetings, evenings on the phone, and other commitments would become commonplace. His wife was in graduate school then and their family time was already at a premium. She encouraged him not to accept the invitation.

He didn't want to hear it. He sulked and grumped, trying to figure out how it could possibly not be something he was called to. It was noble work, it matched his gifts and abilities, and he wanted to do it. He went back and forth for three days between yes and no. Not until he measured the calling against his highest purposes in life was he able to make a decision. His primary purposes were to care for and nurture his wife and children and be successful as a magazine editor. He knew the board position, while exciting, would detract from his purposes at that time in his life. It became clear to him that he was not called to be on the board of the organization—and he declined.

Opportunity ≠ Calling

Opportunities are not synonymous with calling. There are more opportunities in life than any of us could possibly take advantage of. And many people never find their true calling in life because they don't measure opportunities against purpose. If you are doing things without a good reason (purpose), you won't have the emotional and spiritual energy (passion) to sustain the work. Nothing worthwhile in life was ever achieved without a compelling reason to achieve it.

Dr. Howard Hendricks, a well-known professor of theology and leadership coach, said this: your career is what you are paid for; your calling is what you are made for. The goal is to have your career and your calling overlap as close to 100 percent as possible so you get paid to do what you were made to do. Some rare individuals start at 100 percent overlap, but most begin somewhere below 50 percent and spend a few years closing the gap between career and calling.

For instance, if your heart's desire is to travel the world, there are lots of jobs that can help you achieve your dream. Working for an airline is possibly the most obvious. Being a storm trooper (an individual who works for insurance companies assessing the property damage done by hurricanes, tornados, fires, and other natural disasters) or even a missionary will take you places even you never considered.

My granddaughter, Amey, whom I wrote about in chapter eight, was born with wanderlust in her heart. As a young child she would whine, "I want to go somewhere. Anywhere. Can we just go somewhere?" As a teenager she spoke often about how she would one day leave home and how she couldn't wait to get out into the world and see all there was to see. It was a subject she ran into the ground. You can well imagine how it thrilled her when she realized that God's call on her life was a perfect fit for the part of her that craved travel and seeing the world. That inborn desire makes it easier for her to leave her family behind and be about what God has called her to do on the mission field . . . wherever that might be.

Or say you are an aspiring young basketball player. One of the many steps along the way to discovering if you have a future in basketball is to practice. Why should you practice? To do well in the game. Why do you care if you do well in the game? So you can get a college scholarship. Why do you care if you get a college scholarship? Because it will help you get an education to get a good job, or maybe even play basketball professionally. Now, a job or playing professional basketball for a living may be years away. But it is the purpose—the reason—upon which all your efforts are based. Take away the purpose, and all the work to reach your goal becomes wasted effort or could be to no avail. But add the purpose and the hours of dribbling drills, free throws, wind sprints, and conditioning suddenly have a reason. It's the person with his or her eye on tomorrow's purpose (a college education or career in pro sports) who can identify what he is called to do today (trying out for the junior high basketball team).

On a more serious level, why be involved in anything in life that does not help you accomplish your life purpose? Therefore, a key question to ask is: what really matters to you? What "floats your boat," as they say? What do you do when you have free time? What do you dream about doing when you're stuck in a traffic jam? Whatever it is, that's where your heart is; that's what you're passionate about. And somewhere, connected to that passion, is your calling.

We need to become attuned to those moments in life that reveal our values and our passion. It's one thing to identify those moments and take note of what they are saying to us, but it's another to respond to them—to use those moments as a launching pad for action. Sometimes you may not like what you learn about yourself, and that's important too. The important thing is to have your radar on and be in touch with what your heart is telling you about who you are and what fulfills you—and what doesn't—on a daily basis.

Sometimes we resist what may be an obvious calling in our life, not because we wouldn't want to be involved in the final result but because we don't think we can pull it off. I love the story in the Bible of how Moses resisted God's instructions (his calling) for him to go to Egypt and lead the children of Israel out of bondage. It wasn't that he had something better to do. He was one of the most highly educated men in the world, having been raised in the royal family of Egypt, and yet he was working as a shepherd in the deserts of Midian when his call came to him. Nothing against being a shepherd, of course, but Moses was capable of more. But he was fearful of the calling God delivered to him.

Fear can derail even the most exciting calling, and you'll find an entire chapter on dealing with the enemies of the "better than good" life later in this book. You can defeat those enemies just as Moses eventually did. Or you can be defeated by them and never find your true calling in life.

Do you have a dream you would like to fulfill before you die? Ask yourself what is holding you back from making that dream a reality. Is it a God-given dream or a man-driven dream? Have you attempted to make your dream happen and found all the doors closed? Have you asked God to direct your path and show you what He would have you do? Be prepared to wait, but wait with a positive expectation for the answers you seek.

Even if we are content in what we are doing, we should be continually looking for ways we can make an uplifting contribution to our world. We should be asking questions like: What is it that leaves my heart feeling full and my spirit at peace? How can I use my gifts and abilities in a productive and profitable way? How can I move beyond my current level of abilities to make an even greater contribution in the future? What new interests or challenges have come into my life lately to which I need to pay attention? Could they be doorways or pathways to a new and more fulfilling calling? Am I sensitive to things happening around me—those divine interventions that could be signposts or wake-up calls? To what degree am I already fulfilling the highest calling for my life of which I am currently aware?

All of these questions speak to the truth of this wonderful statement from Frederick Buechner: "The place where God calls you is the place where your deep gladness and the world's deep hunger meet."

That is where you will find your purpose—the place where your deep gladness meets the world's needs. Think about what makes your heart truly glad. Then think about the world's needs. To what degree is there convergence between the two? Man's greatest calling comes when he discovers and confirms that what he was put on this earth to do is meeting a genuine need of other people. We discover value and satisfaction in our calling when we can honestly say, "There is nothing I would rather do." The sense of "deep gladness" you get from fulfilling your calling both inspires and energizes you to continue onward, regardless of the personal cost.

Why Are You Here?

We need to get back to the basics of figuring out why we are here. A calling is much more than a vocational expression or function, much more than a job we go to five or six days a week. Calling goes to the very core of our being. If you see your work as a calling, rather than just a job, then it is no longer a toiling sacrifice. Instead, it becomes an expression of you, a part of who you are as a person made in the image of God.

Gail Arnett is vice president of finance at my company, Ziglar Training Systems. I asked him to write down some thoughts on what motivates him and reflect on the sense of calling he feels about his work. I think you'll agree with me that he clearly understands what he has been called to do (Note: Gail is a committed Christian, so he draws inspiration for his calling from the Bible and his relationship with God. While your beliefs might be different from his, you can see how his faith has influenced his sense of calling.):

Mr. Ziglar,

1. Colossians 3:23–24 says, "Whatever you do, work at it with all your heart, as working for the Lord, not for men, since you know that you will receive an inheritance from the Lord as a reward. It is the Lord Christ you are serving" (NIV). The author of those verses, the apostle Paul, says I should do my best in everything I do to please Christ who is going to give me my final reward. Therefore, I should be aware that He is watching all that I do. What greater motivation do I need?

2. I am motivated by the fact that I have been given opportunities through my work, church, and everyday circumstances to have an impact on the lives of others. Whether directly through my own efforts or indirectly by the efforts of others I support, I am continually rewarded by seeing lives changed, by seeing people's needs met.

3. I am motivated by my family. I know I have at least seven people who, like Christ, are constantly watching me to see if I am the man I say I am. I know their lives are being shaped every day, right in front of me, based on my actions, words, and thoughts.

Sincerely,
Gail R. Arnett

When I read that note from Gail, I knew how fortunate I was to have a person like him working with me. He gets it! His calling is to serve the One to whom he believes he will one day give an account for his life, to serve those whose lives are being changed by what he does, and to serve his family by living an honest and transparent life before them so that the next generation will be motivated to seek their highest calling as well.

Pursuing Your Calling

I believe my own life is a good example of what it means to nurture a dream and not let go of it. I don't say that to my credit. Rather, I credit the power that a genuine calling can have in your life!

Twenty years passed between the birth of my dream to be a public speaker and the fulfillment of that dream. During that time I experienced disappointments, frustrations, and, to be honest, considerable discouragement. It's more than just a cliché to say that those with a dream are the ones who keep going when the going gets tough. Not only did I have a dream, the dream had me!

That calling was the motivating factor in my life and I'll be forever grateful that the desire was so strong. I listened to other speakers when I had the opportunity. I read about speaking. I dreamed about speaking. I thought about speaking. And in my imagination, which has always been very active, I saw myself standing in front of audiences that were cheering, applauding, and giving me standing ovations. In my imagination I made literally hundreds of speeches and every one of them was absolutely magnificent! I never stumbled, stuttered, or failed.

T. E. Lawrence expressed it quite well: "All men dream, but not equally. Those who dream by night in the dusty recesses of their minds wake in the day to find that it was vanity: but the dreamers of the day, these are dangerous men, for they may act their dream with open eyes, to make it possible." I actively pursued my dream every working day.

When I realized I wanted to be a public speaker, I was far from God. What He wanted for my life was of no immediate concern to me at all. I moved forward with my dream thinking only of myself and how my family would benefit by my successful speaking career. I wasn't even thinking of those who were supposed to benefit from my brilliant speeches. That's how far from a true calling I was. (Remember Buechner's two parts: our deep gladness and the world's needs. I had the gladness, but I wasn't thinking of the world's needs.)

I still find it incredible that when I did begin a relationship with God, He took the passion I had for public speaking and revealed it to me as a calling. What, you say, was the difference? Purpose, pure and simple. What I had a passion for—public speaking—was without purpose. I didn't know why I wanted to do it other than that it made me feel good.

But when I started using my speaking gifts for God's glory instead of mine, I started seeing everything through God-colored lenses. I realized my gifts were from Him and that I could encourage other people to know Him at the same time I was doing what I loved to do. And I realized that the principles for success I believed in—integrity, optimism, joy, faith, honesty—were His principles, not mine. I came to believe I was called to encourage others as surely as any preacher or scientist has been called to do what they do. I just didn't realize that speaking was actually my calling until I saw it against a larger backdrop—the backdrop of God and His purposes for my life.

And a funny thing happened as a result—something I never expected. When I committed my life to Christ and started studying and teaching biblical principles in my public speaking, my career exploded. And it has been "better than good" ever since.

Standing at the Crossroads

Think back on the happiest moments in the tapestry of your life.

In the thousands of moments that are woven together to make up your story, there are undoubtedly some where time seemed to stand still; where you felt like you were outside yourself, watching yourself doing something truly significant, truly gratifying, truly important. I believe those are the moments in which you find yourself standing at the crossroads of purpose, passion, and peak performance; where those three dynamics merge and become one.

For most people, those moments take on a kind of spiritual quality. They become divine moments in our memories. And I believe they are exactly that—moments in which God reveals that what we are doing is what He'd always planned for us to do; moments in which what we are doing, without question, is pleasing to Him; moments we want to save, and perpetuate, forever.

Most of us have so many distractions, and in some cases so much baggage, that we plow through life unaware of the times when purpose and passion meet and create a broad boulevard named Calling. But I encourage you to begin looking for that crossroads—the place where purpose, passion, and peak perform-ance meet—in your life for His glory and the deep gladness of your own heart.

14 | People and Purpose

We are all in the same boat in a stormy sea, and we owe each other a terrible loyalty.
G. K. CHESTERTON

Your friend is the man who knows all about you, and still likes you.
ELBERT HUBBARD

Greater love has no one than this, that one lay down his life for his friends.
JESUS CHRIST—JOHN 15:13

Fate makes our relatives, choice makes our friends.
JACQUES DELILLE

You can make more friends in two months by becoming more interested in other people than you can in two years by trying to get people interested in you.
DALE CARNEGIE

You can never establish a personal relationship without opening up your own heart.
PAUL TOURNIER

I have yet to see a commercial on television advocating the power of relationships as a way to fight winter colds and flu. Yet there seems to be plenty of evidence to support the idea. A *New York Times* article, "Social Ties Reduce Risk of a Cold," reported:

> Building on a dozen studies correlating friendship and fellowship with health, a new study has found that people with a broad array of social ties are significantly less likely to catch colds than those with sparse social networks. The incidence of infection among people who knew many different kinds of people was nearly half that among those who were relatively isolated, the researchers reported. The lack of diverse social contacts was the strongest of the risk factors for colds that were examined, including smoking, low vitamin C intake, and stress.

A researcher at Duke University Medical Center found that "heart disease patients with few social ties are six times as likely to die within six months as those with many relatives, friends and acquaintances." And Dr. Janice Kiecolt-Glaser, director of health psychology at the Ohio State University College of Medicine, and her husband, Dr. Ronald Glaser, a virologist at Ohio State, reported, "A person's immune response to vaccines increases with the strength of his or her social support."

There you have it—there's power in people!

Better health is only one of an infinite number of reasons why healthy relationships are so important. The poet John Donne had it right: "No man is an island." Unfortunately, some people try to live like they are—isolated from friends and family, thinking them to be more trouble than they are worth.

Sure, people have faults. But so does the person who's looking for a faultless friend. In fact, his greatest fault is the misconception that perfection in relationships exists. The Hasidic rabbis have a saying that is right on when it comes to relationships: "One who looks for a friend without faults will have none."

People who truly understand God's purpose for their lives know that we are all called to be intimately involved with one another. Like cells in the human body, we are only healthy—spiritually, emotionally, and physically—when we are doing our part, squeezed right up next to those we can help and who can help us.

According to Dr. James Merritt, a Gallup Poll revealed that by a count of 10-1 people say they prefer a good relationship with the people they love above corporate position or bucks in the bank. And yet the reality is that they invest most of their emotional energy making those dollars and gaining those corporate positions. Why do people say one thing and yet do another?

Psychiatrist Smiley Blanton said that in his career he had never dealt with a person suffering from dementia, regardless of age, who did three things: stayed active physically, kept learning mentally, and developed a genuine interest in other people.

My friends in counseling professions—ministers, psychologists, psychiatrists, and social workers—say that nearly 100 percent of the counseling they do is because of relationship difficulties: husband-wife, parent-child, teacher-student, employer-employee, neighbor-neighbor, sibling-sibling, and so on. It seems like relationships ought to come naturally, but it is obvious that they don't.

When we come to the end of our lives, it won't be the material things we've accumulated that we'll want surrounding our bed. It will be the people we've loved and those who have loved us in return. Lives of passionate purpose are "others-filled." At the end, if we have lived a "better than good" life, we will have no regrets about the amount of time we have spent with our loved ones. If we do what God has asked us to do by loving our neighbors as we love ourselves, we will never lack for strong, healthy relationships. We don't have to approve of others' lifestyles to be accepting of them and loving toward them. Just think about what God had to overlook in our lives when He reached out in love to us!

Purpose and Marriage

I willingly and proudly go on record (for the umpteenth time) about the cause for the success I have enjoyed in my career as a speaker and trainer: had it not been for The Redhead, it never would have happened. At the human level, she has been the wind beneath my wings. She has been the one to say, "You can do it," when I needed that affirmation from her.

When The Redhead says, "I love you and I believe in you," I'm instantly recharged. I can't begin to tell you what it has meant to me to have a cheerleader like her encouraging me and praying for me every day and every night.

People who want to be continuously motivated and enjoy a "better than good" life need to have the home-court advantage. It's important in basketball, for sure. But the home-court advantage in the NCAA and NBA pales in comparison to the home-court advantage a solid marriage brings.

NBA star Jason Kidd can attest to that. In 2001 Jason Kidd was a wife abuser. He went to counseling, asked for and received help, and the problem was solved. The next season he came very close to being the Most Valuable Player in the NBA and led his team to back-to-back NBA Finals in 2002 and 2003.

What changed a good basketball player into a great basketball player? I think the answer is Jason Kidd's ability to focus on the issue at hand. That's the definition for *genius*. When he is on the basketball court today, all he's thinking about is, *How can I be a better basketball player and lead my team to victory?* When he's at home his entire focus is, *How can I be a better husband and parent?*

I laughingly tell people, "If The Redhead ever leaves me, I'm going with her!" I'm motivated by her and am therefore motivated to make certain she stays around. For instance, when my telephone rings in my office at the house, which is where I do my writing and calling, I answer this way: "Good morning! This is Jean Ziglar's happy husband!" Virtually everyone who calls me at home for the first time comments on that greeting before getting to the reason for their call. The Redhead loves it and I score points with her.

Since the number one cause of a decline in productivity on the job is marital difficulty at home, and since husbands and wives impact each other so dramatically, it just makes sense to acquire and secure that home-court advantage. When you do you will be more successful on the job, which enables you to provide for your family in a more significant way. You will also experience a reduction in financial stress. Then you can enjoy some of the extra things in life that make it better.

Tom Rath and Donald O. Clifton, PhD, reveal in their book *How Full Is Your Bucket?* that if husbands and wives will follow the 5-1 ratio (five positive observations or comments to their mate for every one that is in any way critical or even dogmatic), the marriage has a magnificent chance of being happy and long-lasting. On the other hand, if there is one negative for every positive comment, divorce is virtually a foregone conclusion. Ten years after they did the original study they discovered they had been 94 percent accurate in diagnosing marriage longevity with the 5-1 ratio rule.

Like any newlyweds, The Redhead and I had to learn how to live together when we got married. There are always little things—and sometimes big things—to work out, and fortunately ours were mostly little. But that's not always the case. Cheri and Dean Perry have given me permission to share with you their own experience in going from unhappy to happy in their marriage, and the difference it made.

Following is Cheri's description of their marriage at the time she came to our Born to Win seminar:

When I arrived at your [company's] seminar I thought I was coming to find out about success and mostly to meet

Zig. However, after a short while I realized the real reason I was in Dallas, Texas. My marriage was falling apart. My husband and I had been on two separate ships for many years and divorce was the only real goal we were aiming for together (not intentionally). Even though we are self-employed and work from our home, communication was broken down. Tenderness was a faint memory and sometimes even a kind word was hard to muster. I knew it had to be his fault . . . so when I walked into your seminar I knew HE should have been there—and then something happened! I purchased everything I did not already own at your seminar, but the best investment would have to be the *Courtship After Marriage* tapes.

I listened to them and Dean listened to them and things began to change. We began to get focused and work in the same direction. We began to smile at each other and show our son that mommies and daddies can laugh and love. I was in the grocery store the other day and my son was playing in the play area while I picked up the groceries. When I returned to pick Tyler up, the gal behind the counter asked where my husband was. I said he was at home. She then said the words that I will forever be grateful to you for: "I am getting married tomorrow and I wanted to tell you both that I want to have a marriage just like yours."

The Perrys' marriage changed because they chose to work on it together. Love is a commandment. If it were not, God would not tell us to love our neighbors as we love ourselves. He would have said, "I know your neighbors aren't perfect but try really hard to love them anyway. I hope you can. Good luck." He would not tell us to do something if it were impossible to do.

Passages like 1 Corinthians 13 and Ephesians 5:21–33 in the

New Testament show how we can love one another in marriage, and how marriage can be part of our fulfilling our true purpose in life.

Purpose and Work

To the degree it's possible, you should surround yourself with the wisest people you can—people who know things you don't know, who can pull you up to a level higher than where you are today, who can validate or correct your choices as needed. Because we spend so much time in our work settings, the people we interact with become critically important in life, second only to family.

I have made it a habit to develop relationships with professionals from whom I can gain wisdom and insight in my life, with the intent of passing that wisdom on to others through speaking and writing. I call on Dr. Kenneth Cooper for medical information and advice. Dr. Frank Minirth, nationally known Christian psychiatrist, helps me with psychological information and advice. I go to Fred Smith, my mentor and friend, and the wisest man I have ever known, for advice in all areas of life. I have relationships with respected Christian leaders and theologians including my pastor, Dr. Jack Graham, and Dr. David McKinley, as well as Rabbi Daniel Lapin from the Jewish faith.

The idea that we can grow without surrounding ourselves with those who know more than we do is preposterous. Even if you have to go outside your immediate work environment to find mentors and advisors, I strongly encourage you to do so. If you are trying to fulfill your true purpose in life, you'll only do it with others' help.

Because growth is like the proverbial food chain, everyone is a little further along than someone else. That means you can be a resource, advisor, mentor, or influencer to those younger or less mature than yourself—if you will invest the time and energy in doing so.

The authors of *How Full Is Your Bucket?* reviewed more than ten thousand businesses and more than thirty industries and discovered the following:

- Individuals who receive regular recognition and praise increase their productivity and stimulate increased engagement among their colleagues. These employees are more likely to stay with the organization, receive higher loyalty and satisfaction scores from customers, and have better safety records and fewer accidents on the job.
- More than twenty-two million workers in America are extremely negative or actively disengaged at work, lowering productivity.
- Sixty-five percent of Americans received no recognition in their workplace the year prior to publication of the book.
- Nine out of ten people said they are more productive when they're around positive people.

If you are a business owner, manager, or leader at any level, I hope you saw in those findings some action points to pursue. Part of your purpose in life is to build strong and fruitful relationships with others, and your work setting is a perfect place to start.

A few years ago, our company hired James Howard, founder and president of Honinteg International (note the combination of "honesty" and "integrity" in his company's name), to evaluate the internal workings of our company. I asked him what managers generally do when they have employees who go above and beyond what they are asked or expected to do. I was shocked when he told me that 93 percent of the time they do nothing! No recognition, no rewards, no commendation. No wonder workers are unmotivated!

We use "I like _____ because _____" notes in our company: "I like John Doe because he is always so courteous to everyone." Or "I like Jane Doe because she always has a smile and something nice to say." When you write out a brief note to someone commending him for an action, trait, or accomplishment, you make his day. You can even leave a note with your tip in a restaurant or when someone services your car or repairs your appliance at home. It only takes a minute to encourage someone to "Keep up the good work!" I find that leaving these kinds of notes does as much for me as it does for the person I am encouraging.

Consider making it a daily goal: write one short note, or at least offer a spoken word, to someone each day—especially to a person who is not in a position to return the favor. But even if it is at work, where notes of encouragement can be interpreted the wrong way in this hypersensitive age, figure out a way to be an encourager. You never know who you might be pulling up to the next rung on the ladder to achieving the "better than good" life.

Purpose and Trust

Biblical scholars tell me that the most important theological word in the Old Testament is the Hebrew word *hesed*. It means "loyal love." It's how the ancient Israelites thought of God—as one who could be trusted, one who keeps His promises.

Is anything more valued in the realm of relationships than trust? It is a terrible thing to be in a relationship where trust is violated. If you are the one who fails to be loyal, honest, or dependable, it may take years to restore your credibility. If you are the one whose trust or confidence was violated by another, it may take years for you to ever trust that person again. Outside of love (of which trust is a subcategory), nothing is more valued in another person than trust and loyalty.

And no one can fulfill his or her purpose in life without being trustworthy and loyal. Can you imagine a person who lies or betrays a confidence being respected by his or her peers? Being looked at as a peak performer? Passion, peak performance, and purpose can't exist apart from trustworthiness. Arthur Friedman spoke it well when he said, "Men of genius are admired; men of wealth are envied; men of power are feared. But only men of character are trusted." Logical conclusion: if there is trust in a relationship, it has a marvelous chance of being successful long term.

One of the ways we communicate that we can be trusted is in the way we care for other people. When people see we care for them they will "entrust" their lives (and their hopes, dreams, and fears) to us as a confidant—someone who will treat them and the content of their heart the same way they would treat it. I saw this illustrated in a community in which we lived years ago.

We enjoyed the professional services of one of the most highly skilled surgeons I've ever known. He was recognized locally and regionally as being one of the very best in his field. However, he had a detached, impersonal "bedside manner" when it came to dealing with patients. As a result, he made only a comfortable living and was not terribly successful either socially or financially.

We also got to know his older brother, a general practitioner who worked in the same community. He was a competent physician but in no way enjoyed the reputation for brilliance in his field as the surgeon. Unlike the surgeon, this doctor was much loved by his patients and their families and was highly regarded in the community for his caring manner. He took time with his patients, answering their questions and explaining his treatments. As a result, his practice was booming. He had a great family and was highly successful socially and financially.

The message from the lives of the two doctors is this: it's more important to care *about* people than it is just to care *for* them. Said another way, people don't care how much you know until they know how much you care about them. That's an oft-repeated saying, but it is true and worth putting into practice. It's rare today to find people who know how to devote themselves wholeheartedly to a relationship—to really focus and give themselves totally to a person in a given moment or over a period of time.

A few weeks ago I was getting a haircut from the man who has been my barber for over thirty years. He was interrupted briefly by a phone call, saying it was from a man who wanted to come to work for him as a barber. My friend didn't hesitate to tell the man no and when I asked him why, he explained that the applicant was a smoker. The applicant understood he wouldn't be able to smoke inside the shop, so that wasn't the problem. My barber just didn't want one of his barbers to be constantly thinking about satisfying his craving for nicotine while he was supposed to be focused on giving a customer a quality haircut.

I thought that was a profound insight. Addictions have ruined countless relationships. It doesn't matter if a person is addicted to drugs, sex, gambling, tobacco, pornography, or alcohol—or even shopping, food, or television. Addictions have the effect of dividing our personality in half—one half is devoted to the person with whom we have a relationship and the other half is devoted to satisfying the addiction. We get the feeling that the addicted person is never "all there."

An addict has to put himself first in practical terms. Granted, he or she made the choices that led to addiction, but once the addiction is full force, it owns the person. There is no way to have a healthy relationship with a person who is addicted to anything until the addiction is broken. If you are struggling with any kind of addiction, I encourage you to summon all your strength and reach out for the help you need to put that part of your life behind you. It may be the hardest thing you've ever done for a year or more, but that's a small price to pay for decades of future freedom.

The best relationships are those where there are no distractions and no third parties (addictions) coming between the persons involved. Life can only be "better than good" when you can be trusted. And if you have an addiction you are sustaining you will never be completely trusted.

Purpose and Self

Outside of your relationship with God, the most important relationship you can have is with yourself. I don't mean that we are to spend all our time focused on me, me, me to the exclusion of others. Instead, I mean that we must be healthy internally—emotionally and spiritually—in order to create healthy relationships with others.

Motivational pep talks and techniques for achieving success are useless if a person is weighed down by guilt, shame, depression, rejection, bitterness, or crushed self-esteem. Countless marriages land on the rocks of divorce because unhealthy people marry thinking that marriage, or their spouse, will make them whole. Wrong. If you're not a healthy single person you won't be a healthy married person.

Part of God's purpose for every human life is wholeness and health. I love the words of Jesus in John 10:10: "I came that they may have life, and have it abundantly." God knows we are the walking wounded in this world and He wants the opportunity to remove everything that limits us and heal every wound from which we suffer.

Some wonder why God doesn't just "fix" us automatically so we can get on with life. It's because He wants our wounds to be our tutors to lead us to Him. Pain is a wonderful motivator and teacher! When the great Russian intellectual Aleksandr Solzhenitsyn was released from the horrible Siberian work camp to which he was sent by Joseph Stalin, he said, "Thank you, prison!" It was the pain and suffering he endured that caused his eyes to be opened to the reality of the God of his childhood, to embrace his God anew in a personal way. When we are able to say thank you to the pain we have endured, we know we are ready to fulfill our purpose in life. When we resist the pain life brings us, all of our energy goes into resistance and we have none left for the pursuit of our purpose. It is the better part of wisdom to let pain do its work and shape us as it will. We will be wiser, deeper, and more productive in the long run.

There is a great promise in the New Testament that says God comes to us to comfort us so we can turn around and comfort those who are hurting with the comfort we have received from Him (see 2 Corinthians 1:3–4). Make yourself available to God and to those who suffer. A large part of our own healing comes when we reach out with compassion to others.

My counselor friends tell me that the purpose of all counseling is to get the counselee to change his or her thinking. When we change our thinking we change our life. Two things have to happen in order for thinking to change: we need to accept what is true, and we need to accept it more than once. That is, just as our present patterns of thinking are the result of years of experiences and thoughts, so it will take time to renew our minds. We start with the truth and meditate on (tell ourselves) that truth daily until we develop new and healthy ways of thinking.

From that perspective, "counseling" (receiving truth that changes our thinking) can come in many forms—reading a meaningful book, having a conversation with a friend or mentor, listening to a speech or sermon, attending a play or concert, watching a movie, or listening to inspiring recordings in your car. I have found that God will use a variety of media to "speak" to us—to show us where our current thinking needs to be changed. More important than the means of delivery is our willingness to receive and respond to the truth when we hear or see it. The promise of truth being delivered to us is found in John 16:13: "But when He, the Spirit of truth, comes, He will guide you into all the truth; for He will not speak on His own initiative, but whatever He hears, He will speak; and He will disclose to you what is to come."

Thinking of counseling that way, we can say that life is one long counseling session from beginning to end. I've already said in this book that none of us is perfect, nor will we ever be this side of heaven. Therefore, we all have issues all the time—issues that could hold us back from achieving our purpose in life and achieving higher peaks of performance. Ideally, we should spend our lives counseling (speaking truth to) one another. Of course, that is one of the purposes of God's institution called the church, a place where we "consider how to stimulate one another to love and good deeds . . . encouraging one another" (Hebrews 10:24–25). Sometimes that happens and sometimes it doesn't—but it's the way God intended for each of us to find deeper levels of wholeness along the path we call life. Relationships are nothing more than interdependent people bonding and banding together to encourage one another to be their very best.

Sometimes extreme matters require the help of professional counselors. All too often people don't have the kinds of meaningful relationships by which they can grow stronger and better, and they must resort to paying for the help they need. In this regard, independence is one of the curses of our modern age. Women are told they don't need men. Teenagers are told their parents are idiots and buffoons. Too many children are learning that television and video games are their best friends. We walk around with earphones in our ears listening to music, lost in our own world. Communities, even families, have become collections of intimate strangers. It's no wonder that counseling offices are overflowing with clients and hospitals are filled with people whose physical ailments have emotional roots.

We were not made to live alone. We were made to live at peace with ourselves so we could then live in peace with others. The great writer Pearl Buck put it this way: "The person who tries to live alone will not succeed as a human being. His heart withers if it does not answer another heart. His mind shrinks away if he hears only the echoes of his own thoughts and finds no other inspiration."

Are you committed to a life of continual counseling, growth, and education? Are you committed to a life of consistently receiving truth, of renewing your mind? From what sources do you receive your counseling? Are you reading books by authors who speak wisdom? Are you listening to music and watching movies that have redemptive and edifying themes? Are you involved in a small group or community of people that can offer you support, guidance, and encouragement, and in which you give back that which you have been given? Do you know of professional counselors you can see when needed? Are you asking God for wisdom about life on a regular basis? (He says if you will ask, He will provide [see James 1:5–8].)

People who seek to fulfill their highest purpose in life are those who build and keep winning relationships. There is no better way to do that for a lifetime than to live by the Golden Rule: do unto others as you would have others do unto you. I like to paraphrase that truth this way: you can have everything in life you want if you will just help enough other people get what they want.

That is a philosophy, not a strategy! We don't help others in order to be blessed ourselves. But it rarely happens that we don't get blessed in the process. It's God's law of the harvest: we reap what we sow.

Invest in people and you'll be investing in the "better than good" life. And the returns will be greater than you can imagine.

15 | Change Somebody's World One Act at a Time

People are renewed by love. As sinful desire ages them, so love rejuvenates them.
AUGUSTINE OF HIPPO

To love another person is to help them love God.
SØREN KIERKEGAARD

Love is the only force capable of transforming an enemy into a friend.
MARTIN LUTHER KING JR.

He who reforms himself has done much toward reforming others; and one reason why the world is not reformed is because each would have others make a beginning and never thinks of himself doing it.
THOMAS ADAMS

People need loving the most when they deserve it the least.
MARY CROWLEY

For years, I have been doing something that gives me a great deal of pleasure and that, according to the parents who have communicated with me, has had a big impact on the lives of their children. When I have an appropriate opportunity to spend a moment with a little guy or girl four to seven years of age, I lean forward and tell them this: "Billy, I can do something that very few people in this world can do. Do you know what that is?"

Of course, Billy says, "No."

"I can spot a boy or girl who is a real winner a mile away," I say. "I've never failed at this. And just to make sure I keep my perfect record going, I wonder if you'd let me look you over real good? Would that be okay?"

This time Billy says, "Yes"—not really sure where I'm headed with this.

I then kneel down beside Billy and turn him around slowly in front of me, looking him up and down, all the while saying, "Hmmmmm . . . uh-huh . . . yes, yes. . . ." And then I make my pronouncement: "Billy, there's no doubt about it. I can see it written all over you, my friend—you are a *winner*! And I want you always to remember that. Will you remember that for me?"

This time the answer is an enthusiastic, "Yes!"

"I want you to tell Mom and Dad that Zig says you are a winner! And that I've never been wrong when I've picked a boy or girl to be a winner." Usually, Mom or Dad is standing close by observing this, acting like their child just won the Publisher's Clearing House Sweepstakes.

Pete Hinojosa is community coordinator for the Spring Branch Independent School District in Kingwood, Texas, and is in constant contact with students from preschool to twelfth grade. He stopped by a kindergarten class where the teacher's four-year-old son was one of the students. Like most energetic four-year-olds, the boy was out of his seat, jumping up and down trying to reach a cardboard leaf hanging from the ceiling. Pete was familiar with my

"You're a winner" routine and went over to the little guy. He went through the whole deal, and by the time he finished, pronouncing the teacher's son a winner, the tyke was wide eyed and calm.

As Pete was leaving the classroom he heard the little guy yell to his mom, the teacher, "Hey, Mom, can he really do that?"

"He sure can!" his mom confirmed.

Pete Hinojosa was passing on a little bit of encouragement and affirmation—and changing the world one child at a time!

Life is like a relay race in track and field. The first runner completes his leg and hands the baton off to the second runner, who then gives it to the third, who passes it to the fourth. The smoothness of the handoff has as much to do with the outcome of the race as does the speed of the sprinters.

We do lots of baton passing in life. Parents pass on critical information to their children about faith, love, security, values, and manners. Parents then do a handoff to teachers, coaches, Scout leaders, and others who impart educational, athletic, and service lessons. Then the child, now a young adult, is handed off to college mentors, or perhaps military or vocational trainers, where they learn job skills and additional sets of values and knowledge.

All this time, the way the handoffs and transitions occur is critical. Words of encouragement are like the sticky stuff that is sprayed on the baton to allow each runner to get a firm grip. Sometimes how new information is presented—whether in an encouraging or discouraging fashion—makes all the difference in how it is applied. The world is ultimately changed by the small words and acts that accompany our daily interactions with others.

You, the Philanthropist

What pops into your mind when you hear the word *philanthropist?* Maybe it's people like Microsoft founder Bill Gates who, along with his wife, has given away $28 billion. Or maybe Intel founder Gordon Moore and his wife, who have given away more than $7 billion. Or Andrew Carnegie who gave away 90 percent of his wealth after he retired (and he was the richest person in the world at that time).

When we see those kinds of numbers in the news we immediately dismiss ourselves from the ranks of significant philanthropists. But not so fast! If you look at the Greek root of our English word *philanthropy* (*philos* = "love"; *anthropos* = "man"), it simply means "the love of man." Just because some people get a lot of attention for showing their love for man with gifts of money or property doesn't mean there aren't other kinds of philanthropists in the world—including you and me.

Former British prime minister Margaret Thatcher wisely said, "No one would remember the Good Samaritan if he had only had good intentions." This reminds us that all of us can be, and should be, philanthropists because of our ability to be loving, to do things for the betterment of mankind. We can give something to our fellow human beings that can't be bought: our interest, our love, our time, and our concern. When we encourage, support, and affirm others, we are good Samaritans indeed!

Thousands of people across our country who have modest bank accounts and incomes are philanthropists in the purest sense of the word. They visit nursing homes and shut-ins to talk, play checkers, listen, and be with the lonely and needy. They read books and magazines to the blind. They deliver food with programs such as Meals on Wheels. They contribute regularly to the Red Cross blood drives. They volunteer as candy stripers in hospitals or as a teacher's aide in inner-city schools. They work in homeless shelters and soup kitchens and they visit inmates in prisons and jails. All of these acts of philanthropy are at the heart of the world's need for loving encouragement. They may not land you on the lists of America's largest donors in terms of money, but you will be at the top of the list among those you touch and serve.

Winston Churchill said, "We make a living by what we get; we make a life by what we give."

"But," you say, "I have nothing to give." Wrong. I know of at least one thing you have with you at all times that costs you nothing to acquire or maintain and that has proven to be of tremendous benefit to every person in the world. If I tell you what it is, would you be willing to give it away?

It's your smile.

Researchers have identified nineteen different kinds of smiles, each of them capable of communicating a pleasant message that will often be met with a smile in return. A smile is often interpreted as a positive affirmation, an expression of acceptance or pleasure, and, in many cases, love.

When we encounter a person, we look first to his or her face because that's where the signs of life are. If a person has an animated countenance, we feel positive, expecting good things from the encounter. If the person's effect is negative—the brow is furrowed or the face has a scowl—we're put on the defensive. If the effect is flat, or neutral, we're not sure what to expect.

All it takes to set up the potential for a positive encounter with another person is a smile. You obviously have no control over another person's face, but you do have control over yours. By something as simple as wearing a smile you can raise the likelihood of having a positive, fruitful encounter with another person. And you could produce a smile in them if they are smile-less for whatever reason.

Joseph Addison said, "What sunshine is to flowers, smiles are to humanity." They are but trifles, to be sure, but scattered along life's pathway, the good they do is immeasurable.

Several years ago a study revealed something that most people have known for a long time. After weeks of testing the appearance, personality, and attitudes of subjects and their influence on others, professors at Yale University discovered that a smile is the single most powerful force of influence that people have. That's good news, because all of us can generate enough energy for a smile.

Here's another thing you have to give that can change someone's life if you use it carefully: advice. Several years ago my wife and son and I were having dinner at a restaurant in Dallas. The server came by and sloppily sloshed water into our glasses, pouring most of the ice cubes onto the table. I asked him, "You don't like your job, do you?"

"No, I don't," he replied.

"Well, I wouldn't worry," I said. "I don't think you're going to have to put up with this job much longer."

He stopped what he was doing and asked, "Why not?"

"Son," I said, "there's no place of business in existence that can afford to have someone with your attitude working there—even if you paid them to let you work."

With that, the young man took off from the table in a big hurry and disappeared into the kitchen. Two seconds later, in a scene reminiscent of an old slapstick comedy movie, he emerged through the door leading back into the dining room with a huge smile on his face. It truly was a sight to behold. I watched him as we ate our meal and he was a model employee—pleasant, enthusiastic, helpful, and attentive. As we were getting ready to leave, I called him to the table and gave him a nice tip. He thanked me for the tip—and for what I had said to him. It was obvious that my brief but sincere words changed his thinking and his actions.

You, the Youth Worker

Nothing is more important to the future than the children and young people of today. Everything invested in them now will reap benefits in quantum amounts down the road. And one thing you can give children and young people is an example of what a responsible adult looks like.

When Grant Hill completed his standout college basketball

career with the legendary Duke University Blue Devils, he could have entered the NBA with a big head and an even bigger chip on his shoulder. After all, he was a member of the back-to-back 1991 and 1992 NCAA championship Blue Devils teams, a unanimous first-team All-American pick his senior year, an NCAA All-Tournament pick, and an NCAA Southeastern Regional MVP—besides being the number one draft pick of the Detroit Pistons in the 1994 NBA draft. But pride and arrogance aren't Grant Hill's way (all too unusual in the world of professional sports). He is considered one of the most humble and unassuming members of the pro athlete fraternity. No flashy clothes or gold jewelry or trash talk for Grant Hill—just an elegant authority that speaks volumes about his values.

So where did he learn to live life differently? When his and his wife's collection of African-American art was showcased at the Naismith Memorial Basketball Hall of Fame, Hill described how he was inspired by his dad: "I wanted to be like my father. As a child, our home was filled with paintings, sculptures and artifacts from places throughout the world. . . . It had a profound impact on me and shaped my own thinking about collecting African-American art and sharing my collection."

But it wasn't just his father who impacted the superstar. When he described a particular painting that showed a lone woman standing on the shore overlooking a lake, he said, "I have often said that this work reminds me of my mother. I think of her standing on the shore in her mind as she made the decision to leave her home in New Orleans and attend Wellesley College. It is the moment of truth that is represented in the work that I find so strong."

Grant Hill's examples were a father who provided an environment of art for his family and a mother who struck out on her own to get an education. And then there were athletes: "When I was young," Grant recalls, "I remember watching [the great NBA star]

Julius Erving. The thing I liked best about Doctor J was that he carried himself with class. He never went out of his way to embarrass anybody. I feel like I come from a generation that has the wrong type of heroes. I never got to see Arthur Ashe play tennis, but I saw the way he lived his life after tennis. I always felt that was the type of person I should be looking up to because of his spirit. It's a matter of respect."

Every one of us is a living example to the young people around us. It's not a question of whether we are being watched; it's a question of what the young people are seeing. That which they see, they will reproduce. If you're going to give away your example (and you will), make sure it is one you will be proud to claim years later when you see it reproduced in the life of a young person who watched you.

Ed Shipman and his wife are giving away positive examples of all sorts these days in Granbury, Texas, and it's paying off in spades in the lives of children. The Shipmans founded Happy Hills Farm more than twenty years ago when they took in five foster children. Today, the farm is a widely praised Christian boarding school and working farm for kids with behavioral and academic problems. The faculty and staff (which includes a resident psychologist) oversee five hundred beautifully kept acres. Happy Hills refuses all government aid so as to maintain the ability to teach a faith-based curriculum and worldview. Ed personally takes responsibility for raising the school's $3 million annual budget and contributes to that effort by drawing a modest $45,000 salary as the principal of the school.

Nearly half the food consumed by the students is raised on the farm, and the students dress in uniforms of polo shirts and khaki skirts and pants (with uniforms being passed down to incoming students). The school is fully accredited and licensed in Texas and an average of 70 percent of the troubled, academically challenged students go on to college.

If you think about what those children are lacking when they enter Happy Hills Farm and compare it with what they have when they leave, it's something money can't buy but that the hearts and hands of loving mentors can give.

One of the most meaningful recognitions I have ever received is the Silver Buffalo Award that was presented to me in October 2002. This award, created in 1925, is the Boy Scouts' highest "civilian" honor, bestowed upon those who give noteworthy and extraordinary service to youth. Other recipients have been Lord Robert Baden-Powell, founder of the Scout movement and chief Scout of the world, Charles A. Lindbergh, Norman Rockwell, General Colin L. Powell, *Apollo 13* commander James A. Lovell Jr., Walt Disney, Hank Aaron, Bob Hope, Vince Lombardi, Neil Armstrong, Charles M. Schulz, and thirteen presidents of the United States, among others. I tell you, I feel like I'm in pretty tall cotton when I look at that list! But the reason I feel so privileged by the award is because it is given to those who have impacted young people.

My interest in the development and welfare of young people stems, I am sure, from the number of adults who invested themselves in me when I was growing up. My mother spent her life teaching me about honesty, character, loyalty, integrity, faith, respect, and love. Her example of doing right when doing nothing or doing wrong would have been so much easier has influenced my choices for the full course of my seventy-nine years.

My mother taught me the value of surrounding myself with people who would lift me up, not pull me down. She started by explaining why she wanted me to work for one man and not for another. She knew the job I had and the money I earned would never be as important as the life lessons my boss would teach me. I have already told you about the first man I worked for, Mr. Anderson, the grocer who became my surrogate father and shaped my life as strongly as if he had been my father. John

Anderson loved me like the son he never had, and I needed him more than other boys whose fathers were still living.

Men and women like Mr. Anderson changed my life, one selfless act at a time. Their time was invested in me in school classrooms, the Sunday school rooms at church, the places I worked, the athletic teams I played on, and yes, in the Boy Scout meeting room. I find it most interesting how life goes full circle. The principles I learned in the Scout program are the same ones that, applied to my life, earned me the Silver Buffalo Award.

My work with youth has included developing a program that teaches youngsters how to improve their self-esteem, set goals, plan for a successful life, and make wise choices. The "I Can Course" is taught in schools across the country and it thrills me to meet young businessmen and women who tell me they had the course in school and that it helped them build a better life.

My involvement in the war against drugs put me in touch with a side of life youngsters should never have to experience. It made me see how vitally important it is for young people to have good mentors—people they can look up to who care about them. All the drug programs in the world won't fix a child who doesn't feel loved and worthwhile.

I encourage you to invest time in America's youth, whether in your home, neighborhood, church, or community. After your own children, what about their friends? Do they need extra attention? Are they being supported and encouraged? Ask yourself if you can make a difference for them and then do it. Each act of kindness and investment in time will reward you with blessings untold. Volunteer to teach a Sunday school class, to help on a school field trip, to tutor a slow reader, or to be a Scout leader. If you will make yourself available to God, He will put in your path the young people He wants you to love.

People who change the world and its future are people who give of themselves out of love (philanthropists), especially to those who will populate the next generation (youth workers). You can be both by giving of those things that you have with you every day: love, your example, a smile, an encouraging word, a philosophy, a worldview, a hope for the future.

It takes people who live a "better than good" life to create a "better than good" world. That's the world you can help build if you'll look to do it one act, one person, at a time.

16 | Let Love Be Your Guide

The foremost is, "Hear, O Israel! The LORD our God is one LORD; and you shall love the LORD your God with all your heart, and with all your soul, and with all your mind, and with all your strength." The second is this, "You shall love your neighbor as yourself." There is no other commandment greater than these.

JESUS CHRIST—MARK 12:29–31

Love, and do what you like.

ST. AUGUSTINE

Love talked about can be easily turned aside, but love demonstrated is irresistible.

W. STANLEY MOONEYHAM

I have found the paradox that if I love until it hurts, then there is no hurt, but only more love.

MOTHER TERESA

Effort matters in everything, love included. Learning to live is purposeful work.

MICHAEL LEVINE

What would you do if the son of one of your best friends died following heart surgery? When that happened to Hugh Jones, CEO of Barnett Bank in Jacksonville, Florida, he wanted to do something tangible—something that would make a difference. So he established a memorial heart treatment program to benefit children in need of medical attention. When he discovered there were already programs such as his in place in America, Hugh Jones simply shifted the focus to Korean children in need of heart treatment.

He vividly remembers carrying the first little girl, six-year-old Young Joo Yoo, from the plane and taking her and a seven-year-old Korean boy to his home. Using pictures and pointing, Hugh and his wife did all they could to make the children comfortable in the days before their surgery.

Yoo was admitted to the hospital on Saturday night for her Monday-morning surgery. Unable to sleep, Hugh drove to the hospital at 4:00 a.m. to sit with his little friend until time for her surgery. When the nurses arrived to take Yoo to the operating room her eyes filled with tears and she lifted up her arms to Hugh. Blinking through his own tears, he picked her up and carried her to surgery, hugging her tightly before giving her to the nurses.

"Those three or four minutes changed my life," he said later. "There was a cultural difference between us, a language difference, a color difference, and an age difference, but in those few precious moments I realized none of that mattered. All of that can be surmounted, if there is love."

Since then Hugh and his friends have provided life-saving surgery to seventy children. He also established an unprecedented bank-wide employee volunteer program called the Community Involvement Initiative, and one thousand bank employees contribute over forty thousand hours a year to community projects.

At the end of his famous passage on love in 1 Corinthians 13, the apostle Paul wrote, "But now faith, hope, love, abide these three; but the greatest of these is love" (v. 13). And that's really what the "better than good" life is all about—doing what we are called to do in service of others, dying to self, loving our neighbors as ourselves. And I have never been able to figure out how it's possible to do that without having first come to love God with all our heart, soul, mind, and strength.

Therefore, the "better than good" life is about love—loving God and then loving our neighbor as an expression of our love for God. It's love that fixes things in this world, like Korean kids with broken hearts being "fixed" by the love of a Florida banker and his friends.

The Power of Love

There was a lot of love expressed in this country following the terrorist attacks of September 11, 2001, but nowhere more than in New York City itself. When citizens of New York witnessed their police officers and firefighters going into those World Trade Center towers to rescue people and then never coming out, the soul of the city was touched beyond compare.

In the aftermath of that terrible tragedy, various construction unions in the city estimated it would take up to a year and a half and $1.5 billion to clean up the debris from the two fallen towers. But because of the love New Yorkers felt for their city and those who had lost their lives, the unions banded together (unusual in the competitive atmosphere of New York City) and finished the job approximately six months ahead of schedule and way under budget. They took the attack personally. Their comrades, relatives, and friends had been killed.

When love empowers people, amazing things can happen. The rest of the country followed the New Yorkers' examples of love and sacrifice and opened their hearts and wallets to help heal a great, wounded city.

When my friend Fred Smith's son returned from a trip to

Africa, he told his dad an amazing story. Fred's son had been in a hospital where he had seen an artificial leg, and discovered it had been designed by a man who lived near Dallas. It was revolutionary! The average artificial limb costs upwards of twenty thousand dollars, whereas this one could be had for seventy dollars.

When Fred's son discovered how somebody's life could be changed for seventy dollars, he immediately wanted to help get the artificial legs to the people who needed them. Out of love, someone invented a tool to help the helpless, and someone else responded by getting involved to help distribute that tool. Whether people walk again through a miracle as in Jesus' day or through a seventy-dollar artificial limb, love is the motivation in both cases. There is nothing as powerful as love.

According to Susan Rea, one bright autumn day a few volunteers took a group of young children from underprivileged families to a beautiful park for a picnic. They ate lunch near a large pond where the children could feed the fish. Many of the children had never before been out of their own crowded, treeless neighborhood. They chased each other across the grass in circles until they were dizzy, and then they hovered in an excited group at the edge of the pond to throw in their crackers. Every time a fish splashed to grab a cracker the children shrieked with delight. One small boy in particular was giggling so hard he could hardly stand up.

A dignified, white-haired man, walking with a cane, stopped and smiled at the children's pleasure. Then Rufus, the little giggler, noticed the gentleman and that he didn't have any crackers with which to feed the fish. A moment later the gray-suited elderly gentleman was tossing crumbs to the fish while the little boy in a ragged T-shirt and torn sneakers watched with obvious satisfaction.

That four-year-old child had so little to share and yet shared it so eagerly. The willing human heart finds ways of giving that easily transcend obstacles such as poverty and inexperience. What would happen in our world if we all gave and loved with the innocence and generosity of a four-year-old?

Sunday afternoon, October 30, 1994, at 2:47 p.m., Alexandra Nicole Ziglar made her entrance into this world. Her parents and grandparents were all elated and relieved, since both she and her mother were completely healthy. It has always been my custom to give my children and grandchildren nicknames to identify them in a special way. My other three granddaughters are Sunshine, Keeper, and Little Lover. I decided Alexandra's nickname would be Promise because she holds so much promise for the future.

As I reflected on her birth, I was reminded of the fact that she has two well-educated, committed parents who love each other and who share a tremendous amount of love for her. Alexandra's grandparents feel the same way. Research clearly indicates that when children have both parents to raise them, and other adults such as caring grandparents to look to with trust, love, and respect, they benefit greatly.

I have read that 60 to 65 percent of a child's working vocabulary has been acquired by the age of three, 80 percent of a child's character is formed by age five, and 90 percent of a child's personality is formed by age seven. I knew Promise would be raised around a lot of love and laughter, conversation and family get-togethers, so her personality would get off to a fast start. Promise has all the advantages money can't buy, but love can provide!

I mention these things to remind you of how important loving interaction between parents and grandparents is in the early years of a child's life. God says our children are His gift to us: "Behold, children are a gift of the LORD, the fruit of the womb is a reward" (Psalm 127:3). It is our responsibility to shower them with love so they grow up thinking love is a natural part of life. The only way they will learn to be givers of love as adults is if they have been recipients of unconditional love as children.

And fathers—please love your little girls, especially as they go through the difficult identity-seeking years of adolescence. Dr. Ross Campbell, a brilliant psychiatrist from Chattanooga, Tennessee, says that in all of his years of research and practice he has never known an adult of either gender with a sexual dysfunction who had a father who was kind, gentle, loving, thoughtful, affectionate, considerate, and patient. Because of the nature of my business I've had the privilege of hearing many, many stories of lives changed. Several of those stories include men and women who grew up without the benefit of a loving father, some of whom were emotionally or physically abusive.

Fortunately, the absence of love by one's earthly father can be overcome in time by the love of the heavenly Father. I have heard the stories of many young girls whose self-confidence and sense of worth, lost as a child, was restored when they came to know God in a personal way through Christ. God is everything any of us could ever want or need in a father. He is kind, compassionate, patient, and, above all, loving.

The God Kind of Love

In his beautiful book *Rising Above the Crowd*, Brian Harbour tells the story of Ben Hooper. This story means so much to me I told it in my book *Over the Top*, and I'm going to tell it again here.

Ben Hooper was born in the foothills of east Tennessee to an unwed mother. As a result, he and his mother were severely ostracized by their small community. People would say things when they came to town, and the other children wouldn't play with Ben at school.

When Ben was twelve years old, a new young preacher came to pastor the little church in Ben's town. Almost immediately Ben started hearing exciting things about him, like how loving and nonjudgmental he was, how he accepted people just as they were, and how when he was with them he made them feel like the most important person in the world.

One Sunday, though he had never been to church a day in his life, Ben Hooper decided he was going to go and hear this preacher. He got there late and he left early because he did not want to attract any attention, but he liked what he heard. For the first time in that young boy's life, he caught just a glimmer of hope.

Ben was back in church the next Sunday—and the next and the next. He always got there late and always left early, but his hope grew each Sunday. On about the sixth or seventh Sunday the message was so moving and exciting that Ben became absolutely enthralled with it. It was almost as if there was a sign behind the preacher's head that read, "For you, little Ben Hooper of unknown parentage, there is hope!" Ben got so wrapped up in the message, he forgot all about the time and didn't notice that a number of people had come in after he had taken his seat.

When the service was over, Ben got caught in the crowd and suddenly felt a hand on his shoulder. He turned around and looked up, right into the eyes of the young preacher, who asked him a question that had been on the mind of every person there for the last twelve years: "Whose boy are you?"

Instantly, the church grew deathly quiet. Then, slowly, a smile started to spread across the face of the young preacher until it broke into a huge grin and he exclaimed, "Oh! I know whose boy you are! Why, the family resemblance is unmistakable. You are a child of God!"

And with that the young preacher swatted him across the rear and said, "That's quite an inheritance you've got there, boy! Now, go and see to it that you live up to it."

Many, many years later Ben Hooper said that was the day he was elected and later reelected governor of the state of Tennessee. When you see yourself the way God does, you won't just *know* that you are loved, you'll *feel* loved as well. Nothing can change a life like God's kind of love.

Many years ago a young mother was making her way on foot

across the hills of South Wales, England, carrying her infant son. A blinding blizzard overtook the pair, and the mother never reached her destination. Searchers found her lifeless body, with the baby snuggled beneath her, warm and alive. She had wrapped her outer clothing and scarf around the boy and then covered him with her own body. That baby grew up to be David Lloyd George, Britain's prime minister and one of England's greatest statesmen. Love that gives its life so another can live is God's kind of love.

Patrick Morley, in *Man in the Mirror*, tells about a group of fishermen—three men and the twelve-year-old son of one of the men—who spent a great day salmon fishing in Alaska. When their seaplane took off to take them back to their camp, it crashed into the ocean. Two of the men battled the freezing water and riptides and made their way to shore. But the third man was struggling to help his son, who was not a strong swimmer. The two on shore watched helplessly as the currents swept the father and his son, clutching one another, out to sea.

That father chose not to abandon his son but to stay with him regardless of the cost. He would not leave his son or forsake him to the elements. That's God's kind of love.

When reporters focused almost entirely on the big stories relating to Hurricane Katrina, Lynn Purcell Durham of Ocean Springs, Mississippi, became concerned that many of the incredible tales of love and courage surrounding that natural disaster would never be told. She sat down and recorded the ones she was personally familiar with in an article titled, "The South Will Rise Again." This chapter of *Better Than Good* would not be complete without the part of her story she has graciously allowed me to include here:

My friends' grandparents, who are age 90, are from Gulf Hills, a neighborhood of fine homes that were completely flooded by the 26-foot storm surge of Hurricane Katrina. He is a victim of Alzheimer's disease and she is a tiny woman, who by some miracle was able to get him to swim with her to the safety of their neighbor's roof. He hasn't spoken since the storm and he refuses to leave. So she camps with him in a tent, eating the military rations and meals that the family brings daily. Her love and loyalty to her lifetime mate survives their tragedy. She tells her daughter to leave them be, because he is quiet there as long as no one tries to force him to leave. I fear their time left is short but they are together and that's all that matters to her.

Love that will not desert a loved one is God's kind of love (see Hebrews 13:5).

Let Love Be Your Guide

I close this chapter with a profoundly remarkable story from Beth Moore, the well-known Bible teacher and author from Houston, Texas, that she includes in her book *Further Still.* This event took place several years ago in the Knoxville, Tennessee, airport on April 20.

> Waiting to board the plane, I had the Bible on my lap and was very intent upon what I was doing. I'd had a marvelous morning with the Lord. I say that because I want to tell you it is a scary thing to have the Spirit of God really working in you. You could end up doing some things you never would have done otherwise. Life in the Spirit can be dangerous for a thousand reasons, not the least of which is your ego.
>
> I tried to keep from staring but he was such a strange sight. Humped over in a wheelchair, he was skin and

bones, dressed in clothes that obviously fit when he was at least twenty pounds heavier. His knees protruded from his trousers, and his shoulders looked like the coat hanger was still in his shirt. His hands looked like tangled masses of veins and bones. The strangest part of him was his hair and nails. Stringy, gray hair hung well over his shoulders and down part of his back. His fingernails were long. Clean, but strangely out of place on an old man.

I looked down at my Bible as fast as I could, discomfort burning my face. As I tried to imagine what his story might have been, I found myself wondering if I'd just had a Howard Hughes sighting. Then, I remembered that he was dead. So this man in the airport . . . an impersonator maybe? Was a camera on us somewhere?

There I sat trying to concentrate on the Word to keep from being concerned about a thin slice of humanity served on a wheelchair only a few seats from me. All the while my heart was growing more and more overwhelmed with a feeling for him. Let's admit it: Curiosity is a heap more comfortable than true concern, and suddenly I was awash with aching emotion for this bizarre-looking old man.

I had walked with God long enough to see the hand-writing on the wall. I've learned that when I begin to feel what God feels, something so contrary to my natural feel-ings, something dramatic is bound to happen. And it may be embarrassing. I immediately began to resist because I could feel God working on my spirit and I started arguing with God in my mind. "Oh no, God, please no." I looked up at the ceiling as if I could stare straight through it into heaven and said, "Don't make me witness to this man. Not right here and now. Please. I'll do anything. Put me on the same plane, but don't make me get up here and witness to this man in front of this gawking audience. Please, Lord!"

There I sat in the blue vinyl chair begging His Highness, "Please don't make me witness to this man. Not now. I'll do it on the plane." Then I heard it—"I don't want you to witness to him. I want you to brush his hair." The words were so clear, my heart leapt into my throat, and my thoughts spun like a top. Do I witness to the man or brush his hair? No-brainer. I looked straight back up at the ceiling and said, "God, as I live and breathe, I want You to know I am ready to witness to this man. I'm on this, Lord. I'm Your girl! You've never seen a woman witness to a man faster in your life. What difference does it make if his hair is a mess if he is not redeemed? I am on him. I am going to witness to this man."

Again, as clearly as I've ever heard an audible word, God seemed to write this statement across the wall of my mind: "That is not what I said, Beth. I don't want you to witness to him. I want you to go brush his hair." I looked up at God and quipped, "I don't have a hairbrush. It's in my suitcase on the plane. How am I supposed to brush his hair without a hairbrush?" God was so insistent that I almost involuntarily began to walk toward him as these thoughts came to me from God's Word: I will thoroughly furnish you unto all good works (2 Timothy 3:17). I stumbled over to the wheelchair thinking I could use one myself.

Even as I retell this story my pulse quickens and I feel those same butterflies. I knelt down in front of the man, and asked as demurely as possible, "Sir, may I have the pleasure of brushing your hair?" He looked back at me and said, "What did you say?"

"May I have the pleasure of brushing your hair?" To which he responded in volume ten, "Little lady, if you expect me to hear you, you're going to have to talk louder than that."

At this point, I took a deep breath and blurted out, "SIR, MAY I HAVE THE PLEASURE OF BRUSHING YOUR HAIR?"—at which point every eye in the place darted right at me. I was the only thing in the room looking more peculiar than old Mr. Longlocks. Face crimson and forehead breaking out in a sweat, I watched him look up at me with absolute shock on his face, and say, "If you really want to."

Are you kidding? Of course, I didn't want to. But God didn't seem interested in my personal preference right about then. He pressed on my heart until I could utter the words, "Yes, sir, I would be pleased. But I have one little problem. I don't have a hairbrush."

"I have one in my bag," he responded. I went around to the back of that wheelchair, and I got on my hands and knees and unzipped the stranger's old carry-on, hardly believing what I was doing. I stood up and started brushing the old man's hair. It was perfectly clean, but it was tangled and matted. I don't do many things well, but I must admit I've had notable experience untangling knotted hair mothering two little girls. Like I'd done with either Amanda or Melissa in such a condition, I began brushing at the very bottom of the strands, remembering to take my time not to pull.

A miraculous thing happened to me as I started brushing that old man's hair. Everybody else in the room disappeared. There was no one alive for those moments except that old man and me. I brushed and I brushed and I brushed until every tangle was out of that hair. I know this sounds so strange but I've never felt that kind of love for another soul in my entire life. I believe with all my heart,

I, for that few minutes, felt a portion of the very love of God. That He had overtaken my heart for a little while like someone renting a room and making Himself at home for a short while. The emotions were so strong and so pure that I knew they had to be God's.

His hair was finally as soft and smooth as an infant's. I slipped the brush back in the bag and went around the chair to face him. I got back down on my knees, put my hands on his knees, and said, "Sir, do you know my Jesus?"

He said, "Yes, I do." Well, that figures, I thought. He explained, "I've known Him since I married my bride. She wouldn't marry me until I got to know the Savior." He said, "You see, the problem is, I haven't seen my bride in months. I've had open-heart surgery, and she's been too ill to come see me. I was sitting here thinking to myself, 'What a mess I must be for my bride.'"

Only God knows how often He allows us to be part of a divine moment when we're completely unaware of the significance. This, on the other hand, was one of those rare encounters when I knew God had intervened in details only He could have known. It was a God-moment, and I'll never forget it.

Our time came to board, but we were not on the same plane. I was deeply ashamed of how I'd acted earlier and would have been so proud to have accompanied him on that aircraft. I still had a few minutes, and as I gathered my things to board, the airline hostess returned from the corridor, tears streaming down her cheeks. She said, "That old man's sitting on the plane, sobbing. Why did you do that? What made you do that?"

I said, "Do you know Jesus? He can be the bossiest thing!" And we got to share.

I learned something about God that day. He knows if

you're exhausted because you're hungry, you're serving in the wrong place, or it is time to move on but you feel too responsible to budge. He knows if you're hurting or feeling rejected. He knows if you're sick or drowning under a wave of temptation. Or He knows if you just need your hair brushed. He sees you as an individual. Tell Him your need!

I got on my own flight, sobs choking my throat, wondering how many opportunities just like that one had I missed along the way . . . all because I didn't want people to think I was strange. God didn't send me to that old man. He sent that old man to me.

That story of Beth Moore's says it all—and her final pondering is one I ask myself: how many times have I missed an opportunity to share God's love with someone in need? A child, a stranger, a coworker whose hurt I'm too busy to notice. How many other people were there in that airport who saw the old man's need but who were too embarrassed to respond? How can I develop "ears to hear" and "eyes to see" so I don't miss the opportunities God directs my way—opportunities to be God's hands in this world, to do what God Himself would do?

If we will let love be our guide, we will see and hear like God. Then, if we will be obedient, we will reach out and untangle the difficult situations we come across. And when we do, we will be living the "better than good" life.

May God grant you purpose, passion, and peak performance in everything you do. And may you do it all with His love.

Epilogue: The Promise of a "Better Than Good" Life

In 1973, a man named Gary Kildall wrote the first software operating system for a personal computer, a system he called CP/M. In 1980, IBM was getting serious about developing personal computers—PCs—for what they saw as a huge developing market. They approached Kildall about developing his CP/M system to be used on IBM PCs. The IBM executives, looking to make a deal, flew to the west coast to meet with Kildall to lock in his product as the core of their new personal computers. Kildall, however, was less enthusiastic. Silicon Valley legend has it that he chose to go flying in his new airplane and failed even to show up at the planned meeting with the IBM team.

Frustrated with Kildall's lack of interest, IBM looked around for another software system and discovered Bill Gates, cofounder along with Paul Allen, of a small company called Microsoft. Gates had created an operating system called MS-DOS (that was actually based in part on CP/M), and he eventually inked a deal with IBM to license his software for IBM's personal computers, and eventually about 95 percent of the PCs *in the world*. And the rest is financial history.

Before the dot-com bust in 2000, Bill Gates was worth approximately $90 billion, and he has been the wealthiest person in the world for more than a decade. His Microsoft cofounder, Paul Allen, is currently the third richest. Gary Kildall died in 1994 with a reputation as a brilliant computer programmer but a person who failed to see far enough into the future to take the right steps in the present.

Gary Kildall is not, of course, the only person who failed to see what the future might hold. According to *American Scientist* magazine, Thomas J. Watson Sr., founder of IBM, allegedly said in 1943, "I think there is a world market for maybe five computers." That quote has not been proven to be true, but one that is accurate is a similar statement made around 1951 by Douglas Hartree, a brilliant mathematician at Cambridge University in England. He had built the first "differential analyzers" (precursors to the modern computer) in England. He told an interviewer that all the mathematical calculations that might ever need to be done in England could be handled by three digital computers that were then being built: one in Cambridge, one in Teddington, and one in Manchester. No one else, he said, would ever need machines of their own or be able to afford to buy them.

Three computers sufficient for all of England! It just goes to show, doesn't it, that our ability to predict the future, to anticipate how life might change, is woefully inadequate. And yet if we will only take certain steps today, in light of the future, our lives could be radically different and better. What is even more amazing is how stubbornly we often refuse to take off our blinders when someone from the future returns to talk to us—to tell us how different life is going to be down the road.

Did I get your attention with that last statement? "Who, Zig," I can hear you asking already, "has come back from the future to tell us how life could be? What kind of hocus-pocus are you trying to pull?"

The answer to your question is one you're not expecting:

me—Zig Ziglar. I am writing to you from a place that is twenty, thirty, forty or more years beyond where most of you have been. I am a voice from your future. As I write this book, I am seventy-nine years old—or young, as I like to think of it. I only have so many more speeches and books in me, and I need to say the most important things I know while I have the chance.

That's why I've written this book about passion, peak performance, and purpose—what I choose to call the "better than good" life. The bottom line is, at my age I know more now than I used to. I don't say that presumptuously or pridefully—it happens to all of us. If we are attentive, inquisitive, and, preferably, humble as we go through life, we'll know more near the end than we did at the beginning. And I certainly know more about the "better than good" life now than I did when I first started taking baby steps toward it decades ago. That's what qualifies me to be a voice from your future, sharing what I know now that I didn't know several decades ago.

If I had known then what I know now, I wouldn't have made as many mistakes, I would have accomplished more, and I would have experienced more passion, higher levels of peak perform-ance, with deeper purpose than I have. Mind you, I have no regrets—I thank God for every bit of wisdom He has sent my way and how He has been patient with me as a learner.

But, you have to know about me by now that I love to share, to teach, to communicate, and to prod people forward. And it's in this last section of *Better Than Good* that I want to relate the most important part of this book's message. I believe if you will embrace what I want to tell you, your future will be radically differ-ent—and better! You will not be like those with narrow vision who missed what the future holds. You'll listen to the words of one who has "been there and done that" and incorporate a bit of wisdom into your life *now* so that it can bear abundant fruit in the *future*.

Periodically people ask me what I would change in my life if I could live it over. The answer I learned from a lady many years ago—she said she would not change anything because if she changed anything she might not be where she is now, and she loved where she is. That's my story. I've made many mistakes, but if I changed anything I might not be where I am, and I, too, love where I am because of Whose I am and what His promises to me have been, as they are to you.

That is what I want to come back from your future to tell you: if you will begin today to love God with all your heart, soul, mind, and strength through a relationship with His Son, Jesus Christ, you will not regret your past and you can look forward to your future because it will be "better than good."

Having said that, I recognize that some readers of this book have already made a commitment to Christ and are walking faithfully with Him. And I rejoice with you in that fact. But I also recognize that I speak to a lot of people every year who don't know Christ, who may never enter into the fullness of what I discussed in Part III of this book—purpose—because they haven't yet connected with God through Christ.

And I also recognize that some people are interested in my thoughts on motivation, success, training, and performance, but are not interested in my thoughts on spirituality. And I respect that completely. But for those who will hear me out, I want to tell you how to make that connection with God that will not only change your life on this earth but ensure the kind of life you will spend for eternity.

Beginning in 1972, the changes knowing God made in my life were nothing short of amazing. For the first time, I saw my place in God's grand scheme of things. I knew that God loved me and that He had a plan for my life. Walking in that plan became my purpose.

When I saw my life against the backdrop of God's plan and purpose for me, I understood for the first time that what I was doing up to that point (as a motivational speaker and success teacher) was no accident. It's what I was supposed to be doing! I was exercising the gifts of a gracious God who had blessed me and equipped me to encourage and motivate others to discover their true purpose, live a life of significance, and leave a legacy of lasting value.

And talk about passion! I thought I had a passion for my work prior to 1972. But when I began to see my work as an extension of God's work, there were hardly enough hours in the day for me to accomplish what I wanted to get done—and there still aren't!

I continued doing what I was doing: being a husband to The Redhead, a father to my four beautiful children, an encourager to people through my speaking and seminars. But all with a newfound purpose! And that new purpose gave me greater passion for my work with people than I had ever known, which has led to even higher peaks of performance.

God wanted to increase my ability to do good things in this life—to be successful so I'd be motivated to continue, fulfilled so I could sleep well at night, prosperous so I could be generous, and passionate about living the life I'd been given. And that is exactly what God wants for you. And that's why I concluded this book in Part III talking about purpose—it's the key to turning passion into peak performance.

You see, I believe that my ability to speak, to be enthusiastic, to be motivational, to be encouraging, to use my dry Texas humor to make people smile and enjoy themselves—I believe these are all gifts of God given to me to be used for His purposes. The problem was for many years prior to 1972, I didn't understand that. But I do now—and it's made all the difference in the world.

When I learned that I had been created in the image of God (as have you), I began to see my gifts and abilities as gifts from God. And that's the light I hope you saw yourself in as you read this book. Whether you're a teacher, a business owner, a housewife, an accountant, an attorney, an athlete, a member of the military—it doesn't matter. All that you do, you do because you were created in God's image. Imagination, variety, perseverance, creativity, communication, choice—think of all the attributes that make us the crown of God's creation! We didn't invent these attributes; we received them as resources to spend lavishly as we pursue His purpose for our lives.

Did this knowledge change my life in 1972? It absolutely did. Is it still changing my life today? You are holding in your hands the evidence that it is. Living a life filled with meaning and purpose is a lifelong journey, a road that ends in heaven at an eternal destination. But while we're on this earth, every bend in that road brings new understanding, new wisdom, new ways to apply the truths we are discovering. *Better Than Good* is the strongest effort I have ever made to motivate people to let their passion influence their performance as a result of knowing their purpose.

Dr. Tony Campolo has observed that our past is important because it brought us to where we are today. But as important as the past is, it is not nearly as important as the way you see your future—because the way you see your future determines your thinking today. And the most dramatic impact you can have on your future is by beginning, or renewing, if need be, a vibrant relationship with the God who created you and loves you.

I have told you as honestly as I know how that I am a Christian—a person who believes that Jesus Christ is the Son of God who came to earth to die for the sins of mankind and to make possible a relationship with our Creator God. I also believe the Bible is the divinely inspired Word of God, given by God through human authors to reveal Himself and His plan of salvation to the world.

That terminology is not unfamiliar to most Americans, and it wasn't unfamiliar to me even before I became a Christian in 1972.

After all, I was born and raised in America's Bible Belt where Christianity was part and parcel of southern culture. I was not anti-God, nor irreligious. To be so would have been to deny my cultural heritage. But neither was I a Christian. I was just a well-intentioned human being floating along in the religious stream that dominated the culture I grew up in.

And in that stream, I was as lost as a ball in high grass. I would not have known God if He had approached me on the street and spoken my name out loud. Even though I was familiar with Christian terminology—"get saved," "walk the aisle," "be baptized," "be born again"—I never really gave it much thought either way. I knew I wasn't a pure person but I didn't think I was all that bad either. Truth is, I just didn't think about spiritual things before I got saved.

According to The Barna Group most people are doing at least a little bit of thinking about their spiritual life. Barna's web page titled "Belief: Heaven and Hell" says, "There is a tendency to believe if a person is generally good, or does enough good things for others during their life, they will earn a place in heaven. In 2005 the public decided on the matter: 54 percent agreed, 39 percent disagreed. This represents little change since 2002 when 55 percent agreed and 38 percent disagreed; 1996 when 54 percent agreed and 38 percent disagreed; or 1993, when 56 percent agreed with this notion."

My best figuring tells me there is a better than one in two chance that perhaps you would include yourself in those numbers as a person who believes one gets to heaven by being good.

The problem with this view of spirituality is that it contradicts what the Bible says. We could have a laundry list a mile long of all the good things we've done, many of them for God. We could say we've been a minister or member of a big church, sung in the choir, taught Sunday school, given money to the needy, kept the Ten Commandments, been faithful to spouse and family—any or all these things—and we would still come up short. Why? Because the Bible says that "all have sinned and fall short of the glory of God" (Romans 3:23). In spite of all our good works, "all have sinned." And another verse in Scripture says that to have broken one of God's commands (which all have done) is the moral equivalent of having broken them all (see James 2:10).

I recall a conversation I had with my younger brother not long after I became a Christian. Our mother had passed away, and my brother and I were reminiscing and consoling one another in our grief. I said that I knew our mother was infinitely better off now than she had been during her days on earth, and my brother agreed. He said he knew Mom was in heaven because there had never been a better person than our mother. I agreed with him that our mother had been a fine person, but even so, she was not good enough to gain entrance to heaven.

When my brother reacted defensively, asking what I meant by that, I shared with him what the Bible says, that "all have sinned and fall short of the glory of God." With a look of despair on his face, he told me, "Well, my brother, if our mother wasn't good enough to get into heaven, you and I don't have a chance!" To that I responded, "I agree! But the good news is we can get to heaven the same way our mother got to heaven. That is, she had committed her life to Christ. She believed with all of her heart that He was the way, the truth, and the life. She had confessed with her mouth that Jesus was Lord and believed in her heart that God had raised Him from death, and that's what gained her admittance to heaven." That confession meant she had been born again. Christ Himself said to Nicodemus in their famous conversation, "Unless you are born again, you will not see the kingdom of God" (see John 3:1–8; 14:6; Romans 10:9).

Christianity is not a religion; it is a relationship with a person —Jesus Christ. All the other religions of the world offer their followers justice. If you have done enough good in your life, you will be saved. But only Christianity offers grace—the unmerited favor of God. In spite of our sins, God, by His own loving choice, offers us salvation as a free gift (see John 3:16; Ephesians 2:8–9). Ironically, His offer of grace is based on justice, because our sins were not overlooked or allowed to go unpunished. However, rather than punishing us, God sent His own Son to bear our punishment Himself. When Christ allowed Himself to be crucified for our sins, God's justice was satisfied and He was able to extend the free gift of forgiveness and eternal life to us. Jesus became our substitute.

Once in the early years of my speaking career I was invited to fill in for Dr. Norman Vincent Peale, who was taken ill. The audience was obviously disappointed that they had to listen to me instead of the famous Dr. Peale, but I tried my best to fill his shoes. After my speech, an elderly woman, perhaps a bit hard of hearing, approached me. She didn't fully understand who I was and why I had spoken instead of Dr. Peale, but she had heard me described as a substitute and she asked me to tell her what a substitute was.

I told her a brief story of how, when playing ball as a child at recess in elementary school, one of my friends hit the ball through a window, smashing the pane of glass. A teacher cut out a piece of cardboard as a substitute pane to fill the hole. So, I told her, I was like that substitute pane, filling in for Dr. Peale. Meaning to be kind, she told me, "Well, Mr. Ziglar, not for a moment did I think of you as a cardboard substitute. I thought you were a real pane!"

I managed to suppress my laughter as I thanked her for thinking of me as a "real pane." But seriously, I have always thought of that illustration when considering what Christ did for me. He was my substitute—and yours. God's justice required that someone pay for our violations of His standards. Either we would each have to die for our own sins, or someone could die for us. But that someone would need to be sinless—not guilty of his own sins. The only person who could do that was God Himself. And that is why Jesus Christ came to earth—to be our Substitute—to pay the price you and I could never pay.

As a result, when I die and it comes time for my entrance into heaven, it won't be decided on the basis of whether my good deeds outweigh my bad deeds. It will be on the basis of only one thing: Have my sins been paid for? Have I embraced God's Son as my saving Substitute? Have I received, by faith, God's gift of grace with open hands and heart, not relying on anything in myself to earn my way into heaven, but relying on Jesus alone?

If I can answer yes to those questions, God will welcome me into the heaven He has prepared for all those who put their faith in Jesus Christ. If I can't answer yes to those questions, not only will it mean I missed out on the best possible life on earth, it means I will miss out on heaven's best for eternity.

When Jesus was preparing to leave His disciples He told them, "In My Father's house are many dwelling places; if it were not so, I would have told you; for I go to prepare a place for you. If I go and prepare a place for you, I will come again and receive you to Myself, that where I am, there you may be also" (John 14:2–3). It's been about two thousand years since Jesus said those words, and I can't imagine how wonderful the place He has been preparing for us must be by now. But the only way we will be able to enjoy that future pleasure is by doing today what is necessary to ensure it: embracing Jesus Christ by faith and receiving God's free gift of eternal life. When I do that I will have the opportunity to once again see, and spend eternity with, family and friends who knew Christ and who have preceded me to heaven—especially my beloved daughter who has been in heaven since 1995.

With regard to the future, in some areas of life we are beginning to exhibit more and more wisdom. Every Sunday as The Redhead and I drive to church, we see all manner of people out jogging, rollerblading, walking, and riding bikes. Americans are in the midst of a huge fitness and health revival, and that is certainly a good thing. I'm even doing my best to be part of it as well.

But let's face it—regardless of the shape we are in, statistics show that 100 percent of us die! The body only lives so long, but the spirit lives forever. I am amazed at the number of people I see trying to keep something going that they know will eventually die while giving little or no attention to something that is going to live forever. That is not the wisest way to plan for the future!

I am here from your future to encourage you—no, to plead with you—to accept the free gift of eternal life that God offers mankind by accepting Jesus Christ as your own Lord and Savior. Once your salvation is settled and you begin to learn about the purpose for which God created and called you, you can begin to do your best works every day with a truly singular motivation: to glorify God through your life by loving your neighbor as yourself.

A famous passage in the New Testament says, "For by grace you have been saved through faith; and that not of yourselves, it is the gift of God; not as a result of works, so that no one may boast" (Ephesians 2:8–9). Those verses say we are saved purely by God's grace—His free gift to us. Then, once that happens, we're truly ready for the "better than good" life, which is what the very next verse describes: "For we are His workmanship, created in Christ Jesus for good works, which God prepared beforehand so that we would walk in them" (Ephesians 2:10).

It's those good works we do with passion that lead to peak performance and which come to reflect our understanding of our purpose in this life. Had I known this at an earlier age I would have accepted Christ much sooner than I did. And that is what I want to encourage you to do as well. No life is as good as the life lived in intimate relationship with God. If you are seeking the "better than good" life apart from Him, take my word for it: it can't be found!

If someone had told the early computer pioneers what the future would hold, do you think they'd have done things differently? I'm here today telling you how wonderful your future can be if you will walk into it hand-in-hand with the God who loves you. Don't live with spiritual blinders on! Take the word of someone who did for many years and who doesn't want you to make the same mistake. Make today the first day of the rest of your new life in Christ.

May your life be "better than good" for God's glory and to your own delight!

If you've been wondering how to ask Jesus to be the Lord of your life, I've included a prayer that you can pray. If you believe that Jesus died for your sins and that He rose again, pray this prayer:

> Father, I know that I'm a sinner who needs a Savior, so I ask You to forgive me as I repent of my sins. I confess with my mouth that Jesus is Lord and I believe in my heart that God raised Him from the dead.

If you have accepted Christ as your Lord and Savior, I look forward to spending eternity with you because I believe Acts 2:21, which says, "Everyone who calls on the name of the Lord will be saved." Now, find a church home, a place you can go to fellowship with others who believe in Jesus Christ and where you can learn more about Him. Ask a learned Christian whose wisdom is obvious to mentor you. Read God's Word daily and get ready—you are about to experience the life you can't wait to live.

The "Better Than Good" Life

I am doing "better than good" because I understand that failure is an event, not a person; that yesterday ended last night; and that today is my brand-new day.

I am doing "better than good" because I have made friends with my past, I am focused on the present, and I am optimistic about my future.

I am doing "better than good" because I know that success (a win) doesn't make me, and failure (a loss) doesn't break me.

I am doing "better than good" because I am filled with faith, hope, and love and I live without anger, greed, guilt, envy, or thoughts of revenge.

I am doing "better than good" because I am mature enough to delay gratification and shift my focus from my rights to my responsibilities.

I am doing "better than good" because I know that failure to stand for what is morally right is the prelude to being the victim of what is criminally wrong.

I am doing "better than good" because I am secure in who and Whose I am, so I am at peace with God and in fellowship with man.

I am doing "better than good" because I have made friends of my adversaries and have gained the love and respect of those who know me best.

I am doing "better than good" because I understand that others can give me pleasure, but genuine happiness comes when I do things for others.

I am doing "better than good" because I am pleasant to the grouchy, courteous to the rude, and generous to the needy.

I am doing "better than good" because I love the unlovable and give hope to the helpless, friendship to the friendless, and encouragement to the discouraged.

I am doing "better than good" because I can look back in forgiveness, forward in hope, down in compassion, and up with gratitude.

I am doing "better than good" because I know that "he who would be the greatest among you must become the servant of all."

I am doing "better than good" because I recognize, confess, develop, and use my God-given physical, mental, and spiritual abilities to the glory of God and for the benefit of humankind.

I am doing "better than good" because my faith assures me that when I stand in front of the Creator of the universe, He will say to me, "Well done, thou good and faithful servant."

Acknowledgments

Any time a work of any significance is completed, it is invariably the result of a number of people who worked as a team with the same objective. It's my conviction that *Better Than Good* is a work of significance. For that reason I am delighted to be able to recognize those who made it that way.

First let me thank the most important person in my life, The Redhead—my wife Jean—who has now celebrated fifty-nine honeymoons with me. She is a constant source of ideas, love, encouragement, belief, and conviction and very frequently comes up with the "little things" that make a big difference. But most of all it's her spirit of encouragement that has been vital to me in every phase of my life.

Second, I recognize my youngest daughter, Julie Norman, who is the editor of my books. Little did I dream when she first started working with me that I would receive such huge benefits from her contributions. It's marvelous to be able to depend on someone of a different sex and a different generation, who also happens to love me, and who is very bright and patient. The reality is on occasion I'm a little dogmatic. Julie has the ability to smooth out the rough edges and make my material far more "digestible" without changing one iota of the meaning. Her help on this work was invaluable.

Next I turn to Laurie Magers, my faithful executive assistant for the last twenty-eight years, a person of character and integrity who is the personification of professionalism—one of the most dependable people I have ever known. Her consistency is critically important to me. It is not uncommon for her to fill in important details as well as research necessary information and documentation; her effective and efficient filing and retrieval skills are invaluable. She lightens my burden a great deal, challenges me, makes suggestions that are valid, and makes certain that the message is grammatically correct.

My son Tom Ziglar, who is the president and CEO of our company, is a man of character. He is a hard worker with a creative imagination, keeps a thoughtful, steady hand on the wheel, and leads with integrity. In many ways he is the glue that holds it all together with good decisions and excellent people skills that produce a stable work environment.

Richard Oates, my son-in-law who is married to daughter Cindy and is our COO, is a high-energy sounding board to discuss issues and ideas with Tom. He believes we should have taken action yesterday. Tom thinks we should do it tomorrow; so they talk about it and do it today.

Two other men in our company have been enormously helpful in our everyday operations. Bryan Flanagan has been with me for over twenty years and is our director of corporate training. Krish Dhanam, another of my fellow speakers who has been with us over fourteen years, is in charge of our international operations and does our diversity training and virtually all of the international travel. These two men are true servants at heart; each relieves me of many burdens and keeps up with the minute details of our travel schedule and commitments. Both are men of faith, strong character, and complete integrity. The way they cover the "little things" when we travel together plays a significant role in my peace of mind and enables me to focus on the things I must do when traveling, including the preparation of the presentation I will be making.

I want to thank Bert Newman for expertly handling our production for over nineteen years. He supervises all of our filming and recording projects, handles the details surrounding the production of new programs and materials, and produces commercials and customized audio and video projects all in a timely and professional manner. He is one of the hardest-working people on staff and is very dependable. His coworkers hold him in high regard, recognizing his contributions often by reaffirming, "Bert Newman does whatever it takes to get the job done."

In addition to having a very effective staff overall, our vice president Gail Arnett and his team make certain we are financially responsible in the decisions we make. They keep us up to date and in compliance with laws and requirements to ensure smoothly running operations.

I want to thank Sealy Yates for agreeing to be my literary agent. He has a fabulous reputation, tremendous insights, and wise counsel. He was able to arrange meetings with two well-respected publishers he knew would be effective for us. Each made presentations and both were outstanding. We chose Integrity Publishers for a number of reasons and believe it was the best decision for us.

Part of the Integrity organization is Joey Paul. He is a very insightful, wise, hardworking man. Joey read all twenty–four of my published books and one unpublished book, which Integrity will publish after *Better Than Good* has been out for a few months. As a result of reading all of those books, easily close to ten thousand pages (these books cover a wide range of subjects from sales, faith, personal growth, grief, courtship, family, management, etc.), Joey Paul came to know my heart, mind, and objectives as well as just about anybody outside the people I've worked with for many,

many years—and that certainly includes my own family. He provided a complete analysis of the yet unpublished book and made some valuable suggestions which truly enhanced its impact. For *Better Than Good,* Joey gave us a detailed outline which enabled us to focus on the things we were truly aiming for. His insights were invaluable and saved us a great deal of time in the process. I also believe quite strongly that his input significantly enriched the message we felt was important—even critical—to the value of the book and the impact it will have on others. Joey Paul, I am deeply indebted for your contributions. Thank you very much.

I want to give a special thanks to editor William Kruidenier. William took what we gave him and made it the best it could possibly be. His considerable contributions filled in the cracks and buffed and polished this work until it shone in a way that would have been impossible without his expert touch.

I'm also indebted to the rest of the Integrity team that helped make this book all that it is: Jennifer Day, Leslie Peterson, and many others. You know who you are, and I hope you know how very much I appreciate the role each of you played in seeing this book through from the moment of conception to occupying prominent space in bookstores throughout the world. Thank you.

Our outside consultants and trainers make major contributions when called upon. Our attorneys render very valuable services, making certain we are doing everything exactly as it should be done. These things are critically important to a successful corporate operation, and in the writing of this book each played a part in the overall results. These faithful associates, in addition to others on staff who made important contributions, provide me with a genuine comfort level and help things run smoothly in our daily operations.

Needless to say, there are others too numerous to mention whose roles have been important over the years, doing many things to insure that our business is run in a well-organized manner, keeping our stress level dramatically lower than in most corporate offices. Thanks to all of them I believe *Better Than Good* will glorify God and encourage those who do not know Christ to meet Him, and those who do know Him to recommit their lives to serving Him even more effectively.

About the Author

Zig Ziglar is an internationally known author, inspirational/motivational speaker, and authority on how to have a "better than good" life. His philosophy on life and business—which emphasizes integrity, loyalty, faith, honesty, and character—has evolved into training programs that have changed the lives of thousands of people for the better.

He is chair of the Zig Ziglar Corporation. His most famous quote—"You can have everything in life you want if you will just help enough other people get what they want"—indicates the extent to which his corporation is dedicated to helping people more fully utilize their physical, mental, and spiritual resources.

Nine of Ziglar's twenty-five books have appeared on best-seller lists, including *See You at the Top, Over the Top, Raising Positive Kids in a Negative World, Courtship After Marriage, Success for Dummies, Confessions of a Happy Christian,* and *Secrets of Closing the Sale.* His ability to inspire people from the stage, with audio-recordings, or through the pages of a book has made him America's master of motivation.

Ziglar is the father of four children and has been married to their mother, the former Jean Abernathy—The Redhead—for fifty-nine wonderful years. They reside in Plano, Texas, and are members of Prestonwood Baptist Church where Zig teaches The Encouragers Sunday school class.